Moreton Morre

KT-144-758

FORMING a LIMITED COMPANY

FORMING a LIMITED COMPANY

A Practical Guide to Legal Requirements and Procedures

9TH EDITION

PATRICIA CLAYTON

KOGAN PAGE

Acknowledgement

The forms are Crown copyright and are reproduced with the permission of the Controller of The Stationery Office.

The author acknowledges the kind assistance of Companies House, Cardiff, in the preparation of this book.

While every care has been taken to ensure the accuracy of this work, no responsibility for loss occasioned to any person acting or refraining from action as a result of any statement in it can be accepted by the author or publisher.

First published in Great Britain in 1990
Second edition 1991
Third edition 1992, reprinted with revisions 1993
Fourth edition 1994, reprinted with revisions 1995
Fifth edition 1996
Sixth edition 1998
Seventh edition 2001
Eighth edition 2004
Ninth edition 2006

120 Pentonville Road
London N1 9JN
United Kingdom
www.kogan-page.co.uk

ISBN-10 0 7494 4836 9
ISBN-13 978 0 7499 4836 3

The views expressed in this book are those of the author, and are not necessarily the same as those of Times Newspapers Ltd.

British Library Cataloguing-in-Publication Data

A CIP record for this book is available from the British Library.

Typeset by Jean Cussons Typesetting, Diss, Norfolk
Printed and bound in Great Britain by Bell & Bain, Glasgow

Contents

Need help running your Limited Company?

Limited Company Accounting Services

1st Contact Accounting offers a comprehensive range of professional accounting services for individuals working through Limited Companies. Whatever your accounting needs we can help. We are open long hours to suit, offer face to face consultations & charge a set fee per service so you know exactly how much it will cost beforehand.

Call today to book a consultation and find out how we can help you.

0800 082 0659
www.1stcontact.co.uk
assistance@1stcontact.co.uk

Worldwide.

Can you be more specific than that?

Many IT businesses may look to have much in common. But get to
know them and you discover a world of difference between a
lucrative one-man operation and an international consulting firm.
So why would both bank with us? Is it to do with our respect and
support of difference in business? Is it thanks to our broad perspectiv
gained from being a part of a Group that works across 76 markets
around the world? You be the judge.

Find out more at **hsbc.com/commercial**

Or by calling **0800 633 5610.**

COMMERCIAL BANKING

Issued by HSBC Bank plc. Lines are open 8am to 6pm Monday to Friday (excluding Public Holidays). To help us to continually improve our service ar

Worldwide.

HSBC

The world's local bank

Choosing to put your business in the heart of any key business district sends a strong signal to your customers, your competitors and your staff. Being "where it matters" has been a guiding principal for managed and services office company, Stonemartin plc. They offer five 100,000 sq ft buildings within the heart of London (City), Manchester, Reading, Birmingham and Bristol City Centres.

 But its clients gain far more than an enviable image. On offer is a modern, carefully designed space with a range of flexible workplace solutions, meeting rooms and conference facilities for businesses large and small, as well as the city's first Institute of Directors (IoD) hub, where any of the 55,000 IoD members can touch down and use the WiFi enabled directors room for informal meetings, or simply to work.

Following the example of any good hotel, Stonemartin see the value of first class service, refined comfort and attentive consideration. Stonemartin has adopted the concierge approach having first introduced it into their City of London building. The concierge will have good  local knowledge and a can-do attitude to requests and this service is due to be rolled out across all of its centres as standard.

 The company has been careful to design flexibility into its workplace offer. In a climate where business agility is increasingly important, such flexibility gives its clients' the option to tailor its office requirements to fit the demands of their business. It argues that poorly negotiated lease terms, and a lack of appreciation of the real costs of the workplace tied up in elements like rates, services charges, fit out, IT, facilities management, set up and exit costs, stifle agility for many businesses and leave them carrying a dangerous hidden "contingent" liability in the event of an economic downturn.

For further information please contact Tim Worboys, Sales & Marketing Director Stonemartin on **020 7194 7503**, or visit **www.stonemartin.co.uk**

IP: Investment Portfolio

In today's highly-competitive, knowledge-based economy, protecting intangible assets is becoming increasingly important for start ups and SMEs.

Intellectual property protection in the form of patents and trade marks can bring a number of benefits to young businesses.

Such intangible assets look good on the balance sheet, meaning they are near enough essential when it comes to raising investment capital for SMEs, for which funds can be limited.

Not only can intellectual property help strengthen applications to borrow funds, it can also encourage funding by private investors and shareholders until sales turnover is generated.

Patent Power

Patents are increasingly being used as effective business tools by SMEs. Knowledge and technology-based businesses can generate additional revenue streams from licensing, cross-selling and franchising their technology. A larger company cannot simply copy a patent-protected innovation and may instead agree to pay royalties to the patent holder. This source of income can aid a young business to grow at low cost and low risk.

SMEs can be subject to larger companies imitating their technology without consent and payment, unless they have consistent IP protection.

Trustworthy Trade Marks

Aside from helping new businesses to raise finance, intellectual property can also help to create brand awareness and identity.

Trade marks can help to protect business logos, distinctive packaging and company names and are therefore vital to the identification of products and services in the marketplace.

Once protected, a new business should look to establish a brand presence and compete against other businesses by means of differentiation.

Long term, a familiar trade mark can help to reduce price sensitivity and therefore enable the owner to command a premium price in the market for brand-named goods.

Many SMEs tend to avoid trade mark searches and protection because of their limited funds. However, all too often have new businesses been ordered to shut down as a result of a decision to go ahead without conducting a search, finding out only too late that the name or design already exists.

Accidental infringement of intellectual property is all too common and the only way to avoid this is by simply checking. Just like a patent search, a trade mark search will help to discover another business with the same or similar name or design in question. Conducting searches will cost only a few hundred pounds, but ignoring the issue could cost you your business.

The law allows you to register your rights and protect you from imitators. Speak to an experienced patent or trade mark attorney who can give valuable advice on your intellectual property portfolio and help you to protect your business.

FORRESTER KETLEY & CO

Protecting business identity…

Protecting business ideas…

Protecting what's **yours**.

FORRESTER KETLEY & CO

CHARTERED PATENT ATTORNEYS

TRADE MARK ATTORNEYS

London • Birmingham

www.forresters.co.uk   email: info@forresters.co.uk

NORTH LONDON	**CENTRAL LONDON**	**BIRMINGHAM**
FORRESTER HOUSE	6th FLOOR	CHAMBERLAIN HOUSE
52 BOUNDS GREEN ROAD	105 PICCADILLY	PARADISE PLACE
LONDON N11 2EY	LONDON W1J 7NJ	BIRMINGHAM B3 3HP
Tel: +44 (0)208 889 6622	Tel: +44 (0)208 889 6622	Tel: +44 (0)121 236 0484
Fax: +44 (0)208 881 1088	Fax: +44 (0)208 881 1088	Fax: +44 (0)121 233 1064

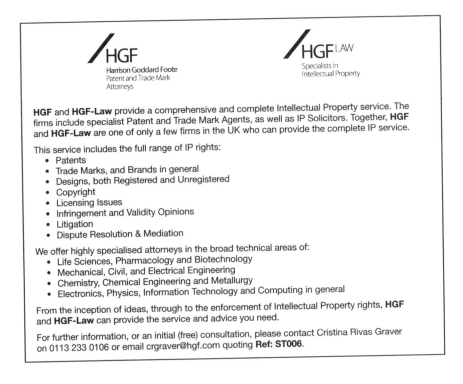

Preface

This is a guide for the aspiring entrepreneur starting in business and for those already running a small unincorporated business looking towards expansion. It explains what a private limited liability company is and the protection and advantages of trading with limited liability.

Chapter 1 describes corporate structure and its advantages and explains the procedure for incorporation and registration. Chapter 2 deals with formation and Chapter 3 covers capital structure. Directors' powers and responsibilities are dealt with in Chapter 4, and Chapters 5 and 6 deal with organisation and administration. Since some consideration must be given to what happens if things go wrong, Chapter 7 summarises the repercussions of insolvency, when the real protection given by limited liability comes into its own, and the final chapter sets out the procedure for buying a ready-made 'off the shelf' company. The English version of the forms and documents regulating company life referred to in the text are reproduced in the relevant chapters.

This book is a guide to incorporation of English and Welsh private limited companies but the Companies Acts apply to Scotland with minor adaptations to take into account the requirements of Scottish law. Company legislation in Northern Ireland and Eire has essentially followed the Companies Acts, including changes introduced by EU legislation.

The law stated is at 30 June 2006 and is based on the Companies Acts 1985 and 1989 and the Insolvency Acts 1986 and 2000, and there are new forms and new fees.

The new Company Law Reform Bill, scheduled to come into force in mid-2007, will make life a lot easier, and according to the Government cheaper, for private companies. Relevant changes are noted in the text and include:

- Dispensing with authorised share capital.
- Directors' general duties, modified to reflect modern business practice, will be specified and they will be able to file a service address with Companies House instead of a private home address.
- Dispensing with a company secretary.
- Shorter and simpler articles of association.
- Simplified requirements for accounts and audits – but annual reporting documents will have to be filed 10 months after the year end instead of 7.
- A choice as to whether or not to hold Annual General Meetings and decisions can be made by written resolution with a simple or 75 per cent majority vote.
- Restrictions on providing financial assistance to potential or actual shareholders to acquire or purchase the company's shares will be abolished and it will be easier to make capital reductions.

This book, however, is intended as a guide, not a blueprint for survival, and you are advised to check with Companies House or take expert advice before forming your private limited company and making major decisions about its future.

Running your own business can be an immensely rewarding experience. Every year approximately 400,000 new businesses start up in the UK. Unfortunately, one in three closes within three years and less than one in five survive 10 years. This statistic should not put you off, but encourage you to plan effectively and seek professional help before you start.

The decisions you make in the early years can be the most difficult as well as the most important, particularly for first time entrepreneurs and those with no previous business knowledge or experience.

In order for your business to succeed, you need to have a good business idea and a clear plan for providing the goods or services that your customers want, at a price they are prepared to pay.

Once you have researched your idea and you have a clear plan of what you are going to do, you need to decide on your business format; sole trader, partnership or limited company?

Limited company

A limited company is a legal entity separate from its owners. A big advantage of this format is its continuity. Ownership can be changed or extra capital raised through the selling of shares without necessarily affecting the management of the company. And if the business grows, the company structure can easily accommodate the expansion.

However, there are many laws and regulations covering the operations of companies, as well as significant tax issues, and these can add substantially to the time and money spent on administration.

To give your business the best possible start, speak to a chartered accountant. It's our job to use our experience to make your business work; we can help you put your plans together and then put them into action. As our members maintain high ethical and professional standards, you know you can count on a chartered accountant.

Visit **www.icaew.co.uk/find** for more information.

When money matters get complicated, find someone you can count on

From tax returns to advice on growing your business, you can count on a Chartered Accountant. Find one at www.icaew.co.uk/find

THE INSTITUTE OF
CHARTERED
ACCOUNTANTS

IN ENGLAND & WALES

Labyrinth Technology
"Guiding you through the maze of modern I.T."

Labyrinth offer a range of technology products and services selected specially for the small business market. We have spent many years building a portfolio that offers only the best quality for our clients.

Two of our web-sites that offer products across the UK are QuickBooksHeaven and CommsHeaven.

www.*QuickBooksHeaven*.com

QuickBooksHeaven offers the full range of QuickBooks software at market leading prices.

"QuickBooks remains the bookkeeping choice for small businesses" *PC Pro, June 2006*

- Create invoices, credit notes and purchase orders
- Collect, track and pay your VAT
- Easily print cheques, pay bills & track expenses
- Track unpaid bills
- View all your customer and supplier data in one place
- Track stock
- Track cash flow

And much, much more!

For more information call us or email **QBH@labyrinthIT.co.uk**

www.*CommsHeaven*.com

CommsHeaven offers top quality business communications for an age where reliability is essential.

- Business Broadband
- Managed Firewalls
- Leased Lines
- VoIP (Voice over Internet)
- Non-Geographic Numbers
- Secure Backup Service
- Internet Usage Monitoring

And much, much more!

For more information call us or email **ch@labyrinthit.co.uk**

Labyrinth Technology Ltd
Unit 34, The City Business Centre, Lower Road, London, SE16 2XB
Telephone: 08707 66 23 27

1

Why a limited company?

Your business structure is crucial to the way you operate: it is the legal framework which determines your share of profits and losses and your responsibilities to business associates, investors, creditors and employees.

CHOICES

You have three options:

1. operate as a sole trader running a one-man business;
2. join up with partners; or
3. trade as a limited liability company.

WHY A LIMITED COMPANY?

Incorporating business activities into a company confers life on the business as a 'separate legal entity'. Profits and losses are the company's and it has its own debts and obligations. The business continues despite the resignation, death or bankruptcy of management and shareholders and it offers the ideal vehicle for expansion and the participation of outside investors.

WHAT SORT OF COMPANY?

The overwhelming majority of companies incorporated in this country are private companies limited by shares; that is, private limited liability companies. During 2005 nearly 1.9 million companies were listed on the Companies Register in England and Wales, with more than 106,000 listed on the Companies Register in Scotland. In the year ended 31 December 2005, 317,300 new companies were registered in England and Wales and 16,200 in Scotland.

The vast majority of registered companies are private companies – at the end of 2005 only 6 per cent of the companies on the Companies Register in Great Britain, ie England, Wales and Scotland, were public companies. The bulk of the companies' legislation, unlike the legislation of most other European Union member states, applies to both public limited companies and small director-controlled family businesses. Private companies cannot offer their shares and debentures to the public but the directors are permitted to retain control by restricting transfer of shares, and some concessions have been made in the requirements for filing smaller companies' accounts and reports. Much of this will change, however, with the passing of the new Company Law Reform Act in mid-2007.

LIMITED LIABILITY PARTNERSHIPS (LLPS) – AN ALTERNATIVE CORPORATE STRUCTURE

LLPs, the latest form of corporate business structure are organised like a partnership, but the partners, called 'members', have limited liability, and the LLP is liable to the full extent of its assets. The members provide the working capital and share profits and the LLP is taxed as a partnership. Disclosure requirements are similar to a company's. The partners have similar duties to directors and the company secretary, including signing and filing annual accounts and putting together the statement of business affairs in insolvency.

Incorporation costs £20 and demand for LLP incorporation has mainly come from existing partnerships, including professional partnerships.

ADVANTAGES OF TRADING AS A LIMITED COMPANY

Although LLPs and companies have limited liability, a legal existence separate from management and their members and have their names protected by registration at Companies House, there remain major advantages in incorporating your business activities in a limited company. These can be summarised as follows:

- It has flexible borrowing powers.
- The company continues despite the death, resignation or bankruptcy of management and members.
- The interests and obligations of management are defined.
- Appointment, retirement or removal of directors is straightforward.
- New shareholders and investors can be easily assimilated.
- Employees can acquire shares.
- Approved company pension schemes usually provide better benefits than those paid under contracts with the self-employed and those in non-pensionable employment. The level of premium that directors can pay is restricted but there is no limit on the overall contributions paid by the company for the directors, although there is a maximum benefit limit imposed by the Inland Revenue Superannuation Fund Office.
- Taxation: sole traders, partners and partnerships pay income tax. Sole traders' and partners' income is taxed as the proprietors' income, regardless of how much profit is retained as working capital, and interest on loans to the business is taxed as their income. Partners are liable personally and jointly for partnership tax and, if a partner dies, the surviving partners are responsible for partnership tax.
- Directors pay income tax and the company pays corporation tax on company profits, and with current rates of tax company profits earned and retained in the business are assessed to corporation tax at lower rates than if income tax were payable on equivalent profits earned by an unincorporated business.

Limited liability

The main and most important advantage of a private company is the protection given by limited liability. The members' – its shareholders' – only liability is for the amount unpaid on their shares. Since many private companies issue shares as fully paid, if things go wrong your only loss is the value of the shares and any loans made to the company.

You can see the advantage if you compare the position of a sole trader with two separate unincorporated businesses and one becomes insolvent. Without Companies Act protection, the solvent business's assets can be claimed by the creditors of the unsuccessful business. With protection, the creditors usually have no claim.

Protection does not, however, extend to fraud, ie knowingly incurring debts the directors have reason to believe the company cannot or will be unlikely to repay. If proved the directors knew or ought to have known the company had no reasonable prospect of avoiding insolvent liquidation they can face disqualification or imprisonment. If the creditors lose money, the directors and anyone involved in the fraud can be liable and their personal liability is without limit. (See also 'Fraudulent trading' and 'Wrongful trading' on page 77.)

Protection of the company name

The sole trader or partnership can put their names on the door and start trading but names are not private property and anyone can use them. Their only real protection is under the trade marks legislation or by taking legal proceedings in a 'passing-off' action for damages to compensate for loss of goodwill.

The choice of both business and company names is restricted. Company names must be registered with the Registrar of Companies and they are protected by registration on the Registrar's Index of Company Names.

Continuity

A company has a legal existence separate from its shareholders. Once formed it has everlasting life. Directors, management and employees can only act as its agent and it is the company itself which owns property and 'signs' contracts. Shares change hands, management and the workforce may change while the company continues trading. However, the sole trader's business dies with him or her and, in the absence of contrary agreement, a partnership is dissolved on the resignation, bankruptcy or death of a partner. The artificially created company, however, is only killed off by winding up, liquidation, by order of the court or by the Registrar of Companies.

Borrowing and shares

You can increase the company's permanent capital base by a new issue of shares and a company has uniquely flexible borrowing powers.

Ordinary shares can be issued for loans, giving shareholders a right to vote and receive a share of profits by way of dividends.

You can issue preference shares in return for loans and defer repayment to a fixed date, the happening of a specified event or by fixing the rate of dividend. Preference shares do not usually give a right to vote at company meetings. The 'preference' signifies the holder's right to payment of interest or dividend and to preferential repayment of share capital before other classes of shareholders if the company is wound up.

Debentures provide permanent additional capital and can be issued to carry a fixed rate of interest under a fixed or floating charge on some or all of the company's assets. Debenture holders have preference with regard to repayment of capital and payment of interest in a winding up, even if the issue carries no charge on the assets.

Your bank may require the company to be secured by a floating charge. The charge 'floats' on some or all of the company's assets as they exist or change from time to time and is unique to corporate borrowings. It can cover stock in trade, book debts, furniture, equipment and machinery, as well as goodwill and other unspecified assets. Its advantage is that the secured assets can be freely dealt with, mortgaged or sold in the ordinary course of business until the interest or capital is unpaid or there is any other breach of the agreement with the lender. The charge then becomes fixed and the lender can appoint a receiver.

Outside investment

There are tax incentives for outside investors in small unquoted trading companies under the Enterprise Investment, Venture Capital Trust and

Corporate Venturing schemes. Here a 'small' company is one with gross assets of up to £15 million immediately before the issue of the shares purchased by the outside investor and £16 million immediately afterwards.

Your search for outside investment might start with contacting the British Business Angels Association (BBAA), the national trade association that promotes private investment in new and high growth potential businesses.

Knowledge transfer partnerships

These are partly government funded and enable your business to work with a research organisation, university or college with relevant business expertise to develop new products, services and processes. There are some limits on sectors and the type of project. You can find partners through specialist knowledge transfer partnership consultants.

Enterprise Investment Scheme

The scheme only applies to new companies and enables a private outside investor to make a minority investment of between £500 and £400,000 per annum or 30 per cent of the company's share capital and to obtain 20 per cent income tax relief on his or her stake. Relief on up to half the amount invested in the first six months of the year to a maximum of £50,000 can be carried back to the previous tax year. The relief is available only during the first three years of the company's business life, or by a self-employed person starting in business or incorporating business activities during the first three years' trading, and usually the investment must be for a minimum of five years. No capital gains tax is payable on disposal of shares after three years if the initial income tax relief has not been withdrawn. If there is a loss you can choose between income tax or capital gains tax relief. The scheme covers most trading, manufacturing, service, research and development, construction, retail and wholesaling business. There are some exceptions, including financial services, overseas companies and investment and property companies. There is no limit on the amount of share capital that can be issued under the scheme but the details are complicated. If conditions are infringed, tax relief is revoked retrospectively, interest being charged on the relief, which is taxed as a loan from the Treasury; investors should therefore take advice before proceeding.

The Venture Capital Trust Scheme

Companies listed on the Stock Exchange under this scheme invest in small higher-risk unquoted trading companies in the same businesses as the Enterprise Investment Scheme. The investor obtains income tax relief at 30 per cent of an investment in new ordinary shares with an annual limit of £100,000. The shares must be retained for at least five years.

The Corporate Venturing Scheme

This is another tax incentive scheme to encourage investment in small higher-risk unquoted trading companies. The investor company obtains 20 per cent corporation tax relief on investments in new ordinary shares held for at least three years. Capital gains tax is deferred if the gain is reinvested in another shareholding under the scheme, and relief is also available against income for capital losses net of corporation tax relief on disposals of shares. The investor's maximum stake cannot exceed 30 per cent and individual shareholders in the small company must retain at least 20 per cent of the small company's share capital. Small companies whose income mainly derives from licence fees and royalties are now included in the scheme if their royalties and licence fees arise from any kind of intangible asset that the company has itself created.

Relief for the investor is safeguarded even if the small company goes into liquidation or receivership.

Changes to the schemes

Small companies with a substantial proportion of income from licence fees and royalties are included in the schemes if that income arises from intellectual property and intangible assets which the company has itself created.

Retaining control

The sole trader and the sole distributor of a single-member private company run their own show, but in a partnership or company the majority rules the business. Protection of minority shareholders under the Companies Acts, however, is hard to enforce and in practical terms is not very effective. Most transactions can be ratified, even retrospectively, by majority vote of the shareholders. If you hold 75 per cent of the voting shares, and act in good faith and in the interests of the company as a whole, the minority shareholders can only question your decisions if they can prove fraud.

You can form, and change existing companies into, single-member private companies, thus eliminating all possibility of shareholder conflict. As sole shareholder your name and address must be set out in the register of members, together with the date of the change and a statement that the company is a single-member company. The sole member exercises the powers of the general meeting and must minute all decisions. Details of contracts between the sole member and the company must also be minuted. Where decisions are not minuted, the sole member is liable to pay a fine but the decision remains valid.

The 1989 Companies Act provides for the incorporation of partnership companies – companies whose shares are wholly or partly held by their employees – but the legislative framework is not yet in place.

Tax

The sole trader, the partner and the director pay income tax; companies pay corporation tax.

The sole trader and the partners are liable personally to the Revenue for tax on their share of business profits. Under the Self-Assessment rules, retiring partners take their tax liability with them and when partners die, their tax liability passes to their estates. Partners are separately assessed to income tax on their share of profits. The partnership, however, has to complete a Partnership (Tax) Return setting out the partnership's profits and losses for tax purposes, and showing how they were divided between the partners.

Self-Assessment to tax is based on the current tax year instead of the preceding year's income. You can 'self-assess' the company's tax bill but you still have to provide accounts drawn up in accordance with the Companies Acts or computations showing how the figures have been arrived at from the figures in the accounts. Less strict requirements will apply to accounts and audits when the Company Law Reform Act comes into force. Tax on profits is paid nine months after the end of the accounting period and shareholders pay tax on dividends as part of their own liability to income tax.

A director's income is taxed at source under PAYE, and interest on loans to the company and share income are included in taxable earnings. There are certain advantages if his or her salary exceeds £8,500 per annum; the first £30,000 of 'golden handshakes' paid ex gratia or as compensation for loss of office is tax free and redundancy payments can be claimed if the company is wound up.

The company is taxed separately for corporation tax on business profits. Capital gains are taxed at the same rate as income, whether or not they are distributed as income. For 2006/07 the small companies' corporate tax rate is 19 per cent on taxable profits between £50,000 and £300,000. No tax is payable on profits up to £10,000. The full rate of 30 per cent is charged on profits exceeding £1,500,000, with marginal relief on profits between £300,000 and £1,500,000.

Capital allowances and various tax incentives for investment in small businesses have made this country a corporate tax haven, so advice should be sought to take maximum advantage of the situation.

There are tax concessions if you incorporate your business and sell it to the company as a going concern in exchange for shares. A further concession extends to an Enterprise Investment Scheme investor's first disposal of shares in your company.

Companies pay capital transfer tax, individuals pay inheritance tax and both pay income tax on capital gains. For the most part, unless your business is very small, a director is better off than a sole trader or partner taking out the same share of profits.

2

Forming a private limited company

Companies must comply with the rules of corporate organisation and management contained in the Companies Acts. These apply to all companies, large and small, public and private, but some concessions are given to smaller companies. It is simpler and less costly in this country than in any other major commercial centre to incorporate your business activities.

Companies Registration Office

The Companies House main offices are in Cardiff and London and there are regional centres in Edinburgh, Leeds, Manchester, and Birmingham. They deal with company registrations and the forms and documentation which the company is required to file in accordance with the companies legislation. There is a great deal of information on their website, companies house.gov.uk. Their CD ROM gives details about incorporation and you can obtain notes for guidance and free statutory forms. The customer care department deals with consumer queries on 0870 333 3636, or e-mail on enquiries@companieshouse.co.uk.

CHOOSING YOUR COMPANY NAME

Describing your business activities through your choice of name is effective and cheap advertising but:

- The last word of the company name must be 'limited' or 'ltd'. If your registered office is in Wales, the Welsh equivalent 'cyfyngedig' or 'cyf' may be used and company documentation must then also state in English that it is a limited company and the information must be displayed at all places where the company carries on business. Charitable or 'quasi-charitable' companies are exempt from this requirement but a 'quasi-charitable' company must indicate on its documentation that it is a limited company.
- The name must not be the same as or similar to one appearing in the Index of Names kept by the Registrar of Companies.
- Certain 'sensitive' words and expressions listed in Appendix 1 cannot be used without the consent of the Secretary of State or relevant government department. For instance, only authorised banks may use a name which might reasonably be understood to indicate they are in the business of banking.
- The name must not imply a connection with the government or a local authority.
- The name must not be offensive, nor must its use constitute a criminal offence.

Application to register the name is made to the Registrar's Cardiff or Edinburgh office. When permission is granted, the name is reserved pending the passing of a special resolution of 75 per cent of the company's shareholders confirming the name. A copy of the resolution must be sent to the Registrar, together with the registration fee. The name is not effective and may not be used until the Registrar issues the Certificate of Incorporation and permission may be withdrawn before it is issued. The directors are personally liable on contracts made on behalf of the company before issue of the Certificate, so you should allow time for the application for conditional approval to be processed as well as for any delay in sending you the Certificate permitting use of the name.

You can search the index of company names at Companies House or on their website free of charge, but it does not show pending applications. If your name is the same as or 'too like' an existing company's, you may be required to change it within 12 months of registration. The time limit is extended to five years if the Secretary of State feels misleading information or undertakings have been given, or assurances given on registration have not been met. He or she can direct a change of name at any time if the name is so misleading as to the nature of the company's activities that it is likely to cause harm to the public.

Electronic incorporation via incorporation agents is increasingly popular. The agent guides you through registration and there is less paperwork. You can incorporate your company and file documents electronically yourself but you must first register as an Electronic Filing Presenter.

Most company information is filed free of charge and some fees are reduced. When the Company Law Reform Act comes into force companies will be able to communicate with shareholders electronically. You can also file documents via e-mail but this is mainly helpful to big companies that file documents daily or weekly.

Electronically filed information about capital and shareholders is noted in Company House records and updated in the electronic annual returns. Paper-filed information is recorded but not updated in future annual returns.

The PROtected Online Filing service (PROOF) protects the company against fraud and the Companies House Monitor Service within Companies House Direct (CHD) keeps you up to date with statutory filing requirements. Details of these services are on the Companies House website.

THE CONSUMER CREDIT ACT 1974

Registration of the name does not imply acceptance for the purpose of this legislation. You can find out if the business requires to be licensed under the Act on the Office of Fair Trading's website, www.oft.gov.uk, or by contacting the OFT's licensing branch at Fleetbank House, 206 Salisbury Square, London EC46 8JX (tel: 020 721 8608) to check if the name is acceptable to them. Application forms can be downloaded from their website and are also available from your local trading standards department.

TRADE MARKS

Acceptance of your company name does not mean that it can be used as a trade mark. To ensure that you do not infringe anyone's trade mark rights you should search the appropriate class of goods and services at the Trade Marks Registry or the Trade Mark Enquiries Section, Concept House, Tredegar Park, Cardiff Road, Newport, South Wales NP10 8QQ. The Central Enquiry Unit can be contacted by telephone on 08459 500 505 or on their website, www.patent.gov.uk.

Trade mark rights give an automatic right of action against the infringer. Use of an unregistered name may expose you to the risk of a 'passing off' action but compensation is then payable only if the plaintiff can prove that the public has been confused.

The search for a trade mark is technical and you are therefore advised to use a trade mark agent. Details can be found at www.itma.org.uk, www.cipa.org.uk or www.patent.gov.uk.

TRADING NAMES

The restrictions on your choice of trading name are set out in Appendix 1. Otherwise almost any name is acceptable provided it is not misleading or, unless you have the consent of the Minister or relevant department, does not imply a connection with the Royal Family, government or local authority, or national or international pre-eminence.

DISPLAYING THE COMPANY'S NAME

All company documents and stationery must carry the company's full name; its registered number and the address of its registered office must also be included on the company's letterhead. The name must be prominently displayed at the principal place of business and engraved on the company seal (see page 107). It must not be abbreviated or amended, for instance by changing 'X & Co Ltd' to X and Company Limited'. It must also appear on company cheques, payment then being made 'for and on behalf of the company'. Cheques without the company name are the personal liability of the signatory.

AT BECK GREENER we do much more than simply protect new ideas. Our comprehensive professional service and in depth experience enable us to guide you from initial concepts to commercial success.

Intellectual property protection is of paramount importance to any business. We provide expert advice based on a wealth of experience in the field. We always aim to give the best professional service whether we are dealing with the individual inventor or a major multinational.

We protect inventions from simple mechanical toys to complex new drug formulations requiring global protection. We protect famous brands worldwide,

New ideas need expert protection if you want them to soar

nd we help start-ups to identify and protect a name r logo with the potential to become a famous brand f the future.

The UK's role in Europe continues to develop and he European aspect of our work becomes ever more mportant. All of our patent partners are experienced uropean patent attorneys and represent clients lirectly before the European Patent Office.

imilarly, we act directly at the Office for Harmonzation of the Internal Market (OHIM) obtaining and lefending Community trade marks and designs.

f you require professional services in the field of ntellectual property, we can help. Please contact

one of our partners: For trademark matters contact Ian Bartlett. For patent matters contact Jacqueline Needle.

BECK GREENER

Established 1867

PATENT & TRADE MARK ATTORNEYS

Beck Greener, Fulwood House, 12-13 Fulwood Place, London WC1V 6HR.
Telephone: +44(0)20 7693 5600 Fax: +44(0)20 7693 5601.
Email: mail@beckgreener.com **Website: www.beckgreener.com**

IT'S MY COMPANY NAME – WHY CAN'T I USE IT?

JONATHAN SILVERMAN, of Patent and Trade Mark Attorneys, BECK GREENER, says investigate before you choose a company name.

If I had to tell you the most useful thing I learnt at Law School it was this;

> *"Just because you have a company incorporated as Fabtools Ltd, WHATEVER YOU DO…DON'T think you can trade as FABTOOLS!!"*

The Registrar of Companies may allow you to *register* a name for your company, but that does not mean that you are free to use it. *Use* of a trade mark or trading name is regulated by a set of laws that exist outside the rules regulating the choice of a company name. These are the laws of passing-off and registered trade mark infringement.

The law of passing-off protects a business against misrepresentations which are likely to damage its goodwill. Owners of registered trade marks have rights to prevent others using marks which are identical or similar to the registered trade mark.

A competitor with rights to the same or a similar name can take action to prevent you trading using your chosen name, and has a wide range of remedies which include injunctions, damages and an order for repayment of his or her legal costs. In an emergency situation an injunction can be granted quickly to preserve the position pending trial.

It is not a defence that you were not aware of the competitor's prior rights nor that you have a later company name registration.

If you have to change your name you will have wasted marketing effort and have to start again. You will incur the costs of the name change, including choosing a new name, reprinting stationery, packaging, advertising and promotional material.

So in deciding on a company name investigate at the outset whether the proposed name is likely to infringe the rights of others. To avoid incurring professional fees on clear non-starters, you can use an incremental approach starting with some research of your own, as set out below. Remember that the primary objective of this research is to avoid conflict with your competitors. If the results look dangerous then it is usually better to choose another name rather than incur expense.

If things look reasonably clear then you should seek expert advice from a trade mark attorney who can conduct searches of the UK and other relevant trade mark registers and provide you with a detailed report as to the risk you might face in using the name. Such professional advice is not expensive as compared with advertising and similar costs and will be money well spent if it enables you to avoid a costly mistake. The trade mark attorney will also be able to advise on the trade mark protection you should seek and the costs involved.

Remember that company names are only one type of trade mark. You should adopt the same strategy prior to using any trading name, brand, trade mark or logo.

Jonathan Silverman is a trade mark attorney with **Beck Greener**.
Tel: 020 7693 5600   mail@beckgreener.com   www.beckgreener.com

To investigate the marks your competitors use:
- **Look at telephone directories and The Yellow Pages.**
- **Look at trade magazines and journals.**
- **See if the .co.uk; .com domain names have been registered and if possible visit the websites.**
- **Put your name of choice into internet search engines.**

Then seek advice from a Trade Mark Attorney.

DOCUMENTS TO BE COMPLETED

The following documents must be completed and sent to the Registrar, so that incorporation and registration can be effected:

- The printed Memorandum of Association, signed by at least two promoters or the promoter of a single-member company – the 'subscribers' to the Memorandum – who write opposite their names the number of shares they have agreed to take. They can take up any number of shares. Their full names and addresses must be given and their signatures attested by one or more witnesses, giving their full name, address and occupation. Minors, that is persons under the age of 18, should not subscribe as they can repudiate the shares on or before majority. Other companies can subscribe by having a director or secretary sign on their behalf but this should be clearly stated by the signatory signing 'for and on behalf of' the corporate member.
- The printed Articles of Association dated and signed by the subscribers to the Memorandum, their signatures again being witnessed.
- A Statement of First Director(s) and Secretary and Intended Situation of Registered office (Form 10 – see page 22). You must give details of the officers, and directors must give their dates of birth, full name and current address. Company officers can, however, apply to the Secretary of State for a Confidentiality Order permitting them not to reveal their usual residential address on company documents, provided they can show that disclosure would expose them to actual or serious risk of violence or intimidation. The application costs £100 and details are available from the Company Law and Investigations Directorate, 1 Victoria Street, London SW1H 0ET (tel: 020 7215 0225) and the DTI's website, dti.gov.uk. Officers will no longer have to apply for permission to file a service address instead of their private address when the Company Law Reform Act comes into force. The first director(s) and secretary must sign and date the form of consent to act. The form must also be signed and dated by the subscribers to the Memorandum or by an agent acting on their behalf. Private companies will not be required to have a company secretary when the new Company Law Reform Act comes into force.
- A Declaration of Compliance with the Requirements on Application for Registration of a Company (Form 12 – see page 25),

signed and dated by the proposed director or secretary named in Form 10, or by a solicitor dealing with the formation of the company. The declaration must be sworn before a Commissioner for Oaths or a solicitor having the power conferred on a Commissioner for Oaths, or before a Notary Public or Justice of the Peace. They must also state the place where the declaration was made and date the form.

The completed forms must be sent to the Registrar with the registration fee of £20. A same-day service for incorporation and registration costs £80.

It is at this stage that the proposed name is checked. Subject to approval of the name, the Certificate of Incorporation giving the date of signature and the registered number of the company is issued which must be put on all documents sent to the Registrar.

As from the date of issue of the Certificate, the subscribers form a body corporate – the new company – which exercises its own powers. Prior to that date, however, the company has no existence, so that any business contracts already agreed are the personal responsibility of the signatories.

THE MEMORANDUM OF ASSOCIATION

The company's constitution is contained in two documents: the Memorandum and Articles of Association. The Memorandum sets out the company's basic constitution and its powers and duties as a legal entity. The Companies (Tables A to F) Regulations 1985 (SI 2000 No 3373) as amended, available from The Stationery Office, give a standard form of Memorandum and Articles. Draft forms for both the Memorandum and Articles of Association suitably modified for use by a private limited company can be obtained from law and specialist stationers, which can be further modified for your purposes before you apply for registration.

The Memorandum of Association must state:

- *The company's name:* unless it is registered or re-registered with unlimited liability, the last word of the name, if it is trading for profit, must be 'limited' or 'ltd' or the Welsh equivalent. A Welsh company can file its Memorandum and Articles in Welsh, together with an English translation; you should check with Companies House to see if an English translation is still required.
- *That the registered office is in England, Wales or Scotland* (London, Cardiff or Edinburgh is also acceptable): this establishes the company's domicile. Unless you can show that management and control are elsewhere, this means that the company operates under British law and pays British tax.

  The registered office need not be the place at which you carry on business and it is often convenient to use your accountant's or solicitor's address. It is, however, the address to which important and official documents are sent, including service of legal proceedings, so it is important to receive prompt notification of receipt of any documents.

  The address must be filed with the Registrar when you start business or within 15 days of incorporation, whichever is the earlier date. It can be changed, provided you stay in England and Wales or in Scotland, but the Registrar must be notified within 15 days of the change.

  The registered office address, the place of registration and the company's registered number must be put on all business documentation.
- *The objects for which the company is formed:* this clause sets out the objects for which the company is incorporated and specifies its powers. If the company pursues any other objects or goes beyond the specified powers, it is acting ultra vires (beyond the powers of) the company.

  Under the 1989 Companies Act a general commercial company can state that the object of the company is to carry on any trade or business whatsoever *and* that the company has power to do all such things as are incidental to the carrying on of its trade or business. This is sufficient on the basis that the validity of any act done by the company 'shall not be called into question on the ground of lack of capacity'. However, the legislation has not yet been tested in the courts and it may therefore be advisable to include provisions similar to those required under the earlier law, which require the

Figure 2.1 Statement of first director(s) and secretary and intended situation of registered office

Company Secretary (see notes 1-5)

Company name	

NAME *Style / Title [ ] *Honours etc [ ]

* Voluntary details

Forename(s)	
Surname	
Previous forename(s)	
Previous surname(s)	
Address	

Usual residential address
For a corporation, give the registered or principal office address.

Post town	
County / Region	Postcode
Country	

I consent to act as secretary of the company named on page 1

Consent signature [ ] **Date** [ ]

Directors (see notes 1-5)

Please list directors in alphabetical order

NAME *Style / Title [ ] *Honours etc [ ]

Forename(s)	
Surname	
Previous forename(s)	
Previous surname(s)	
Address	

Usual residential address
For a corporation, give the registered or principal office address.

Post town	
County / Region	Postcode
Country	

Day Month Year

Date of birth [ ][ ][ ] **Nationality** [ ]

Business occupation	
Other directorships	

I consent to act as director of the company named on page 1

Consent signature [ ] **Date** [ ]

Figure 2.1 *continued*

Directors (continued) (see notes 1-5)

NAME	*Style / Title	*Honours etc
* Voluntary details	Forename(s)	
	Surname	
	Previous forename(s)	
	Previous surname(s)	
Address		
Usual residential address For a corporation, give the registered or principal office address.		
	Post town	
	County / Region	Postcode
	Country	

Day   Month   Year

Date of birth	Nationality
Business occupation	
Other directorships	

I consent to act as director of the company named on page 1

Consent signature		Date

This section must be signed by
Either

an agent on behalf of all subscribers	Signed	Date
Or the subscribers	Signed	Date
(*i.e those who signed as members on the memorandum of association).*	Signed	Date
	Signed	Date
	Signed	Date
	Signed	Date
	Signed	Date

Figure 2.1 *continued*

Companies House
— for the record —

*Please complete in typescript,
or in bold black capitals.*

CHWP000

12

Declaration on application for registration

Company Name in full

I,

of

† Please delete as appropriate.

do solemnly and sincerely declare that I am a † [Solicitor engaged in the formation of the company][person named as director or secretary of the company in the statement delivered to the Registrar under section 10 of the Companies Act 1985] and that all the requirements of the Companies Act 1985 in respect of the registration of the above company and of matters precedent and incidental to it have been complied with.

And I make this solemn Declaration conscientiously believing the same to be true and by virtue of the Statutory Declarations Act 1835.

Declarant's signature

Declared at

Day   Month   Year

On

❶ Please print name.

before me ❶

Signed   **Date**

† A Commissioner for Oaths or Notary Public or Justice of the Peace or Solicitor

Please give the name, address, telephone number and, if available, a DX number and Exchange of the person Companies House should contact if there is any query.

Tel

DX number   DX exchange

Companies House receipt date barcode

This form has been provided free of charge by Companies House.

Form revised June 1998

When you have completed and signed the form please send it to the Registrar of Companies at:
Companies House, Crown Way, Cardiff, CF14 3UZ   DX 33050 Cardiff
for companies registered in England and Wales
or
Companies House, 37 Castle Terrace, Edinburgh, EH1 2EB
for companies registered in Scotland   **DX 235 Edinburgh**

Figure 2.2 A declaration of compliance with the requirements on application for the registration of a company

company's objectives and powers to be set out in full. 'To make a profit' is implied but everything else must be specified.

The *objects clause* is divided into a number of sub-clauses. The first covers the main business activity and should state clearly and fully all the businesses and activities that it is anticipated the company will undertake. The second sub-clause is usually a 'mopping up' clause which covers any other business which in the opinion of the directors may advantageously or conveniently be carried on in conjunction with the company's main business.

If, however, the company has been formed for a specific money-making venture, this is its main object. If it does not produce a profit and you have included nothing else, the company must be wound up. The objects clause can be changed but only to extend or vary the approach to the specified business activities, to restrict or abandon them, or to sell out to another company. Alterations must be approved by a special resolution of 75 per cent of the shareholders and can be cancelled by the court on the application of a minority of share and debenture holders within 21 days of the resolution.

It is therefore advisable to include everything you might wish to do, setting out several possibilities and stating that any of them can be the main and independent object of the company, in order that your search for profit can be flexible. The standard form is by including a clause stating that 'every object shall be considered a separate and independent main object and none of the objects specified shall be deemed to be subsidiary or auxiliary to any other'.

Following sub-clauses enable the company and the directors to:
– buy, sell and lease property;
– construct buildings, plant and machinery;
– borrow and lend;
– acquire patents;
– issue shares and debentures;
– purchase shares in other companies;
– enter into partnership and acquire other businesses;
– sell the undertaking of the company;
– draw bills of exchange and negotiable instruments;
– establish associations and clubs to benefit directors and employees;
– distribute property to members; and

– do all such other things as may be deemed incidental or conducive to the attainment of the main objects.

The directors cannot borrow or invest on behalf of the company unless they are given the power to do so in the *objects clause*, so it should be framed to give the widest possible powers. They can also be authorised to make charitable, political or other contributions, although it is advisable to impose some control on excessive philanthropy and speculation by providing that no director can act without the approval of a majority of the board.

However wide your *objects clause*, some acts and transactions may still be ultra vires the company and of senior management. Since entry into the EU, however, transactions with third parties acting in good faith and not specifically aware of a restriction bind the company which can, in some circumstances, turn to the director or senior employee for compensation.

■ *That the liability of the member(s) is limited:* this means that if the company is insolvent, the shareholders are liable to creditors for only the amount still owing on their shares; if they are paid for in full, they have no further liability. This applies to all the shareholders, including directors and management, although they may have a separate liability to the company as officers.

If the company continues trading for more than six months with only one shareholder, he or she has sole liability for company debts incurred during that period if he or she knows he or she is the only shareholder.

■ *The amount of initial nominal (or authorised) capital and how it is divided into shares:* this clause states the capital, how it is divided into shares and the nominal value of each share, usually £1.

The percentage of the capital subscribed in cash or asset value is called the issued share capital. Any balance remaining unpaid is the uncalled capital and the shareholders' liability is limited to this amount if the company goes into liquidation. References to share capital in the company's letterhead must quote the issued/paid-up amount, not the nominal figure.

Class rights, attaching to different classes of shares (see below), may also be set out in the Memorandum but are usually set out in the Articles.

■ *The name(s) of the subscriber(s):* if you intend to trade as a single-member company, yours is the only signature required as subscriber to the Memorandum in the *association clause*. The *associa-*

tion clause states that you want to be formed into a company and you agree to take out the shares. If there are to be two or more shareholders, at least two of them must sign the Memorandum stating they agree to take out at least one share each.

THE ARTICLES OF ASSOCIATION

The Articles deal with your internal organisation, the company's relationship with shareholders and their relationship with each other, the issue of share capital, the appointment and the detailed powers of directors and proceedings at meetings.

You will be able to adopt shortened and simplified Articles when the new Company Law Reform Act comes into force. The current 1985 Regulations, however, contain a set of 118 standard Articles designed for public as well as private companies, so they are usually adopted with modifications. For instance, you may wish more specifically to define and restrict the directors' borrowing powers by requiring that loans over a specified amount must be approved by the majority of the board.

Classes of shares

You may want to divide shareholdings into several classes of shares, with different rights attached to each class. The ordinary shares usually carry voting rights and a share of profits (payable as dividend) but shares can be issued carrying increased voting rights or priority in right to dividend or repayment of original capital if the company is wound up. The Articles can set out how rights can be altered or new rights or classes of shares created and, unless they state otherwise, the changes can then be made by passing an ordinary (majority vote) resolution.

Restrictions on issue of shares

The existing shareholders have a statutory right of pre-emption, that is, the right of first refusal, over most new share issues, so they must first be offered to the existing shareholders *pro rata* (in proportion) to their holding at a specified date. The shareholders must be notified in writing of the offer which must be open for at least 21 days. Your private company's Articles, however, can instead give the directors a discretion on allotment of shares (refer to the standard Articles contained in Table A of the Companies (Tables A to F) Regulations 1985 (see page 20)). If the directors are given authority to allot shares, their authority must be renewed five years from the date of incorporation or from the date of adoption of the Article.

Restriction on share transfers

In order to retain control, directors of private companies usually want to restrict the transfer of shares. This must be done by adding a special provision to the standard Articles, which normally provides that the directors may, at their discretion and without having to give a reason, decline to register any transfer of shares.

Often a right of pre-emption (right of first refusal – see above) is also given to the existing shareholding when a member wishes to sell his or her shares. The appropriate Article will set out the detailed procedure for the offer and refusal, including time limits and the method of valuation, with recourse to arbitration if a price cannot be agreed. It should be carefully drafted at the outset because, although the Articles can be changed, it may be more difficult to agree the terms at a later stage. The small family company's directors' domestic problems can have a drastic effect on business decisions and you may also have to consider the interests of outside shareholders.

The basic decision is whether or not the directors should be able to block transfers within and outside the family during a shareholder's lifetime and afterwards, and much depends on the personal circumstances of the promoters.

Purchase by the company of its own shares

Companies can now buy their own shares and assist anyone else to buy them, provided the company's assets are not thereby reduced or, to the extent of the reduction, the finance comes out of distributable profits, that is, profits available for payment of dividends.

Table A includes this provision but the procedure is complicated and there are tax implications, so professional advice should be sought before you take action.

It will be easier for private companies to make capital reductions when the Company Law Reform Act comes into force, and there will no longer be restrictions on providing financial assistance to actual and potential shareholders to acquire or buy the company's shares.

Directors

First directors are named in the statement filed on registration and the Articles usually set out the method of electing subsequent directors, and specify the maximum and minimum number of directors. Table A specifies a minimum of two but a private company may operate with one director, although he or she may not then be the company secretary.

Anyone can be a director of a private company, provided that he or she is not a bankrupt or disqualified from acting as a director under the Insolvency Act. In Scotland the Registrar will not register a director under 16. There is no minimum or maximum age restriction in England and Wales but infant directors must be able to sign the required consent to act and you should take legal advice if you want to appoint someone very young. Some foreign nationals cannot be directors and you should check with the Home Office Immigration and Nationality Directorate, Lunar House, Wellesley Road, Croydon CR9 2BY (tel: 0845 010 5200) or check the website www.ind.homeoffice.gov.uk before appointing a non-British director. The Articles usually disqualify anyone who is of unsound mind or who is absent from board meetings for more than six months without consent. A company can be a director of another company; directors need not hold shares but the Articles can provide that they be required to hold a specific shareholding.

Usually a third of the directors retire and stand for reappointment by rotation each year but the Articles can make provision for life-time directorships.

The Articles covering directors' appointment and removal, however, can be changed by ordinary (majority vote) resolution of the shareholders. The resolution overrides any service agreement made between the director and the company, although the director can claim compensation for loss of office on breach of the agreement. The director's position can be safeguarded by giving him or her sufficient special voting rights on shares owned to outweigh the votes of other shareholders.

For Innovation

Patents
For Inventions

Copyright
For Creative Works

Designs
For Appearance

Trade Marks
For Brands

 A DTI SERVICE

www.patent.gov.uk

Total Business Article

One of the most difficult and sensitive issues related to Intellectual Property (IP) is, "how can I protect my idea when I need to discuss it with others in order to commercialise it?" With certain areas of IP i.e. patents and designs, it is essential that the idea is new and not already in the public domain in order to be granted formal protection. In other areas the creator runs the risk of the idea effectively being stolen if they disclose it to others.

The ideal situation would be for the creator to formalise the protection of their idea before disclosing it to others. This can be done through obtaining a patent for inventions, a design registration for the appearance of a product and trade mark registration for business names, brand names and logos.

If, as is regularly the case, the work can not be formally protected before disclosure to others, the creator should consider the following methods of protection.

Copyright is an automatic right to protect creative works from being copied. The creator should evidence the date on which the work was first created and use the copyright symbol with their name and date of creation on all work that will be viewed by others.

Always ask third parties to sign confidentiality or non-disclosure agreements before disclosing the idea. This may provide avenues to take legal action through breach of contract.

Trade Secrets can be used instead of patents if the final product does not indicate the process that created it. This could provide long term protection, as unlike a patent, the invention will not be published and does not have a fixed term of protection.

Unregistered trade marks provide protection under the common law tort of passing off. This protection is limited in comparison to a registered trade mark and can be very difficult to prove.

Design Right is an automatic right that covers the shape and configuration of a product. As it is automatic, the creator will need to provide evidence to prove the date on which the design was first created.

Finally, the Patent Office would advise anyone embarking on a business collaboration involving IP, to establish a written agreement stating who will own the IP and who will have rights to use it.

For more information contact the Patent Office at **www.patent.gov.uk** or phone our enquiry team on **08459 500505**.

Directors' powers

Directors run the company on behalf of the shareholders. Directors usually exercise their powers through resolutions passed at board meetings. In larger companies the board deals with general policy; day-to-day decisions are left to the managing director and committees of directors. The smaller company works in the same way but in practice decisions are often made by all the directors on a daily basis.

Table A provides that the directors manage the business. They can, as stated in the Memorandum, exercise all the powers of the company to borrow, mortgage company property and issue securities. You can, however, add a provision which limits the total debt the directors can raise without the shareholders' prior consent.

Directors' salaries

Directors' remuneration and their expenses must be authorised by an appropriate provision in the Articles. Table A provides for payment of such remuneration as the company may by ordinary resolution determine, and payment of travelling, hotel and other expenses properly incurred in connection with attendance at directors' and company meetings. Directors are advised also to agree a full service contract with the company, covering salary, share of profits and/or bonuses and reimbursement of expenses to safeguard their position.

General provisions

Other standard articles cover, for instance:

- the company's lien on shares for the balance unpaid;
- making calls on members for moneys payable on shares;
- forfeiture of shares where calls have not been paid;
- meetings, notice of meetings and procedure at meetings, including voting procedure; keeping of minutes and appointment and removal of officers; declaration and payment of dividends;
- winding up; indemnity of directors and use of the company seal (see page 107).

The 1989 Companies Act dispensed with the need for a company seal. The signatures of two directors, or a director and the company

Companies House
— for the record —

88(3)
(Revised 2005)

Please complete in typescript, or
in bold black capitals.
CHWP000

Particulars of a contract relating to shares allotted
as fully or partly paid up otherwise than in cash

Note: This form is only for use where the
contract has not been reduced to writing

Company Number

Company name in full

gives the following particulars of a contract which has not been
reduced to writing

1	Class of Shares (ordinary or preference etc)			
2	The number of shares allotted as fully or partly paid up otherwise than in cash			
3	The nominal value of each such share			
4a	The amount of such nominal value to be considered as paid up on each share otherwise than in cash			
b	The value of each share allotted ie. the nominal value and any premium			
c	The amount to be considered as paid up in respect of b			

continue overleaf

Signed

Date

*Delete as appropriate

** A director / secretary / administrator / administrative receiver / receiver /
official receiver / receiver manager / voluntary arrangement supervisor

Contact Details
You do not have to give any contact
information in the box opposite but if
you do, it will help Companies House to
contact you if there is a query on the
form. The contact information that you
give will be visible to searchers of the
public record.

Tel

DX number   DX exchange

Companies House receipt date barcode

This form has been provided free of charge
by Companies House.

08/2005

When you have completed and signed the form please send it to the
Registrar of Companies at:
Companies House, Crown Way, Cardiff, CF14 3UZ   DX 33050 Cardiff
for companies registered in England and Wales   or
Companies House, 37 Cast e Terrace, Edinburgh, EH1 2EB   DX 235 Edinburgh
for companies registered in Scotland   or LP - 4 Edinburgh 2

Figure 2.3   Particulars of a contract relating to shares allotted as fully
or partly paid up otherwise than in cash

5 If the consideration for the allotment of such shares is services, or any consideration other than that mentioned in 6,7 or 8 below, state the nature and amount of such consideration, and the number of shares allotted

6 If the allotment is a bonus issue, state the amount of reserves capitalised in respect of this issue

7 If the allotment is made in consideration of the release of a debt, e.g., a director's loan account, state the amount released

8 If the allotment is made in connection with the conversion of loan stock, state the amount of stock converted in respect of this issue

Figure 2.3 *continued*

secretary, signing for and on behalf of the company has the same effect as if the document had been executed under seal. Your standard Articles will require use of a seal and, at the time of writing, the only evidence of title to a share certificate is a certificate executed under seal. An alternative scheme to abolish share certificates so that title can be transferred via computer accounts is not yet in operation.

DUTIES AND FEES PAYABLE

A fee of £20 is payable to the Registrar of Companies when lodging documents on formation and the fee stamp is affixed on the Memorandum of Association. Same-day incorporation costs £80.

INCORPORATION

The company exists from the date that the Companies Registration Office issues the Certificate of Incorporation, which is numbered, dated and signed. The name can be changed after incorporation for £10 but not the registered number, so if you want to trace a company you should quote the number.

PRE-INCORPORATION CONTRACTS

You can contract for the benefit of your not-yet-incorporated company, but the company must be specifically identified in the contract by name or description. On incorporation, the company has the same rights and remedies under the contract as if it had been a party to the contract.

If, however, you are still at the organising stage, you may prefer to contract on your own behalf as promoter of the still-to-be-incorporated company. You are then personally liable until the contract and should therefore contract on the basis that you will cease to be liable once the contract is put before the board or general meeting on incorporation, whether or not the company adopts the transaction. Once it is adopted, the contract is replaced by a draft agreement, which is executed by the company after incorporation.

TRANSFER OF EXISTING BUSINESS TO YOUR COMPANY

You can sell your business to the company for shares issued at par (face value). Assets and liabilities are taken over by the company and no capital gains tax is chargeable provided the only payment is the issue of shares.

A formal transfer agreement should be executed transferring existing assets and liabilities to the company on incorporation, but professional advice should be sought as to the tax and legal aspects of transfer. It is advisable to provide a proper valuation of the assets transferred, although you are not obliged to do so. You should formally disclose details of the transactions to shareholders even if this is a formality at this early stage when the company may have only one or two share-holders. Full details should be put on file and the sale should be properly minuted when the transaction is adopted at the first general meeting.

The sale agreement or prescribed form of details of the sale and Form 88(3) – see page 34 – must be lodged with the Registrar within one month of the transaction. A stamp duty of 15 per cent ad valorem (according to value) is payable on transfer of some assets including goodwill and some debts. There is no charge to duty if the total consideration does not exceed £60,000 and the agreement contains a Certificate of Value, which certifies that 'the transaction hereby effected does not form part of a larger transaction or a series of transactions in respect of which the amount or value or aggregate amount or value of the consideration exceeds £60,000'.

Duty of 1 per cent applies to transactions between £125,001 and £250,000 and 3 per cent to transactions between £250,001 and £500,000. The Certificate must state the transaction is within the relevant limits. No Certificate of Value is required for transactions over £500,000; duty is increased to 4 per cent. Stamp duty of 0.5 per cent is payable on the purchase of stocks and shares.

When setting up a company, you need to prioritise your approach to intellectual property, having regard to the nature and scope of the business. Protecting all possible IP in all possible countries would be prohibitively expensive. If you are a technology based research and development company, patent protection will be your main focus. If you intend to trade in consumer products where branding and packaging are important, you may concentrate more on registered trade marks and registered designs.

Whatever the nature of the business, you need to get off to a good start. Registering a company does not guarantee that you will be able to use the company name in connection with your intended business. It is important to investigate what other company names are already in use in a similar line of business, what trade marks are registered and what domain names are in use. A trade mark attorney can assist in the process of choosing a name that is free for use and that you can register yourself as a trade mark, if that is appropriate for your business.

As a new company, you may not be able to fund a worldwide trade mark registration programme of your own. Even so, you should check that there are no obvious trade mark conflicts in major territories. When Apple Computer started up in the US thirty years ago, a trade mark check would have revealed that the Beatles had registered the trade mark Apple in many other countries. As Apple Computer's activities began to extend round the world, trade mark disputes arose. To settle the matter, Apple Computer had to undertake to keep out of the music field, but then found it impossible to comply. In 1991 Apple Computer had to pay over $20 million for a settlement enabling them to continue with their music activities. There are still doubts as to what they can and cannot do, as the recent i-Tunes dispute shows.

Faced with a trade mark conflict, most new companies would not be able to afford substantial legal fees and settlement payments. They would be forced to change their name. This can be a disruptive process for a company that is just starting to find its feet.

For a technology company, an affordable patent strategy is important. A patent attorney can take you through the pros and cons of different routes and help to establish a patent programme that is best for you. It is important to be realistic about the costs and to budget for them from the outset. It may be possible to start the patent process for a modest outlay, but eventually international patent protection is going to be expensive.

As a new company, it is unlikely that you will be suing competitors immediately. For research and development companies, patents provide a basis for transferring or licensing technology. For a manufacturing company, a patent provides a deterrent even if it may be a few years before rights can be enforced. However, one of the most important benefits of patent protection is that it reassures backers that their investment is protected. Some investors will insist that there is patent coverage.

When setting up a company to exploit your idea, there are two possibilities for the ownership of IP. You can transfer IP to the company, or you can retain ownership yourself and grant an exclusive licence to the company. An advantage of the latter route is that if the company becomes insolvent, you will retain ownership of the intellectual property. However, many investors will insist on IP being owned by the company rather than licensed.

Frank B. Dehn & Co. is one of the leading firms of patent and trade mark attorneys in Europe, with offices in London, Oxford, Brighton and Munich. Founded in 1920, we have many years' experience in protecting the intellectual property rights of our clients, be they multinational corporations, SMEs or sole traders. For sound, commercially aware advice on your IP needs, contact us at: **Frank B. Dehn & Co., St Bride's House, 10 Salisbury Square, London EC4Y 8JD;** Tel +44 (0)20 7632 7200, Fax +44 (0)20 7353 8895, mail@frankbdehn.com or visit our website for further information **www.frankbdehn.com**

CODDAN CPM LIMITED

From England to the US, Mauritius to Hong Kong, Belize to Panama, we are one of the leading companies in the industry of International Business Incorporation.

We provide

- a new-business incorporation service which offers same day company formation,
- a fast, hassle free application process,
- competitive prices.

➢ We offer professional assistance and advice in the areas of business establishment, development, financial planning, increasing finance, corporate recovery, payroll, and personnel services.

➢ Working worldwide, we specialise in the incorporation of Private Companies, Public Companies, and Partnerships in England, Wales, Scotland, Northern Ireland, and the Republic of Ireland; Sociedades Limitadas (SL) and Sociedades Anónimas (SA) in Spain; Corporations (Inc.) and Limited Liability Companies (LLC) in the United States. We also incorporate international business entities in offshore locations, and hold a portfolio of ready-made companies which are ready to trade.

In addition to the incorporation of your company, Coddan provides other services such as:

Business structure and pacification • Legal advice • Nominee Director, Nominee Secretary, Nominee Share holder • Registered Address • Virtual office (telephone numbers, fax numbers, office space etc) • Notarizations • Apostilles • Name Registrations • Trademarks • Business Bank Accounts • VAT Registration • Accounting • Web services (design, host)

For more information go to:
www.ukincorp.co.uk or email **info@ukincorp.co.uk**
freephone **(0) 800.081.1510**

3

Capital

The limited liability company is structured for expansion. Once incorporated, your business easily assimilates additional participants and capital and you can retain control as the majority shareholder.

CORPORATE CAPITAL

The company can build up a complicated capital structure and a whole range of special terms describes capital contributions.

When the Company Law Reform Act comes into force you will not need to have authorised share capital. There will be no restrictions on giving financial assistance to actual and potential shareholders who want to acquire or purchase company shares and it will be easier to make capital reductions.

Initial capital contributions

When two directors each contribute £400 to form a company with a nominal or authorised capital of £1,000, each taking 500 shares with a par or nominal value of £1 each, that £800 is the company's paid-up capital for 1,000 shares in the company. The balance of £200 outstanding is the uncalled capital. This can be called on by the company at any time, in accordance with the terms of the Articles, unless it is later decided (by special resolution) to make all or part of it reserve capital which is only called on if the company goes into liquidation.

Nominal capital is the total amount of share capital which the Memorandum authorises the company to issue and any reference to capital on business documents must refer to the issued paid-up capital.

Shares

Your contribution of capital gives you a right to a share of distributed profits but it does not necessarily fix the proportion to which you are entitled.

Payment can be in cash or in kind, including goodwill, know-how or an undertaking to do work or perform services for the company or a third party.

The ordinary shares issued on incorporation give you a claim to income on equal parts of the company's net assets. If you later issue preference shares, their preferential rights must be met before the ordinary share dividend is paid.

INCREASING THE COMPANY'S CAPITAL

You can increase the company's nominal capital by issuing more shares if this is permitted by the Articles. The issue must be authorised by resolution of the company in general meeting in accordance with the relevant Article. If there is no provision for a new issue, an appropriate Article can be added (by special resolution of three-quarters of the shareholders).

The new capital can be by issue of ordinary, preferred or even deferred shares, paid for on instalment terms. If the Memorandum does not permit this, however, you will have to vote on an appropriate amendment.

Notice of the increase must be sent to the Registrar within 15 days of the passing of the resolution, together with a copy of the Minutes of the Meeting, the authorising resolution and the printed amended Memorandum and/or Article.

CHOOSING YOUR COMPANY'S NAME AND TRADING STYLE

When you are setting up your business, one of the first things you need to do is to give it a name. This will be your company's brand or trade mark.

Trade Marks protect the various means of identification by which a product, goods or services, are distinguished from other traders. They are used to identify a particular brand or manufacturer and thereby provide protection for the goodwill and reputation a company has established in its goods and services.

Choosing a good trade mark at an early stage is vital. Your company's reputation rests on its brand and a strong trade mark is invaluable. Many trade marks adopted are unregistrable or conflict with prior registrations. You should not use a trade mark without first getting expert advice on its registrability and having a search conducted for prior rights.

The UK Patent Office offers a free search facility for trade marks on its website but this is extremely limited and can in no way compare with a full clearance search conducted by experts such as those at Prentice & Matthews. Indeed the UK Patent Office website contains a disclaimer to that effect on the relevant page. The Patent Office free search may tell you whether a mark is not free for use or registration but it will not tell you if a mark is available or registrable.

A full clearance search provided by Prentice & Matthews will tell you not only whether your trade mark is free for registration but, perhaps more importantly, whether your proposed use will infringe an existing registration. If you are sued for trade mark infringement the cost to your business, in terms of damages, destruction of infringing goods or material, an injunction against continued trade, legal costs and the subsequent costs of re-branding and re-marketing, could be huge and may even put you out of business.

The process of achieving registration of your trade mark can be complex and sound advice will save both time and expense. Trade mark registration has two benefits. The first is that your trade mark will be put on the Register of Trade Marks at the UK Trade Marks Registry and this will serve as a warning to others that you have rights in that trade mark. You also have the right to sue other traders for infringement of your trade mark if they use the same or a similar trade mark in respect of the same or similar goods and/or services for which your trade mark has been registered. The second benefit is that if you have a (UK) registered trade mark, you cannot infringe anybody else's registered trade mark. (Please note, however, that the existence of a registered trade mark does not automatically confer protection against passing off but honest traders should have no fear in that regard.)

Prentice & Matthews also offer full services for protection and enforcement of patents and designs and can offer advice on copyright issues. Contact them for your specific requirements.

Prentice & Matthews
Calvert's Buildings
52B Borough High Street
London, SE1 1XN

Tel.	**020 7403 8565**
Fax.	**020 7403 8566**
e-mail	**info@prenmatt.co.uk**
website	**www.prenmatt.co.uk**

Pre-emptive rights

Existing shareholders have pre-emptive rights to new issues in proportion to their shareholding. This is the case unless this is excluded in the Articles, payment is not in cash, or the shares carry a fixed dividend, or the directors are authorised to allot the shares.

Directors' authority to allot shares

The directors' authority to allot shares must be contained in the Articles or granted by the shareholders by an ordinary majority resolution in general meeting. It can be conditional or unconditional and lasts for a maximum of five years, renewable for a further five years.

Rights attached to shares, including the right to dividend, depend on the terms of the company's Memorandum and Articles. If you attach the right to vote at general meetings to only one class of shares, the company can be given a wide capital base but management retains control.

Once rights are attached to shares, whether by amendment to the Articles or otherwise, rights can only be varied by the consent of the shareholders affected, however small the group.

If the Memorandum prohibits changes in class rights, you need all the shareholders' consent to a change. If they refuse, you may be able to make changes by using a 'scheme of arrangement' (see page 121).

Details of some share issues carrying special rights which are not stated in the Memorandum or Articles must be filed with the Registrar within one month of allotment. It is therefore advisable to seek specialist advice if you are considering such issues.

Preference shares come in all guises but they all have some preference over other classes of shares in their right to dividend and/or repayment of capital.

Preference dividends are paid at a fixed percentage rate on the price of the share before anything is paid to ordinary shareholders. You can issue several classes of preference shares, ranking one behind the other in their right to dividend. Their dividends are cumulative unless the Memorandum or Articles state that they are not, so that arrears must be paid before the ordinary dividend is paid. If they are stated to be non-cumulative, a dividend passed is a dividend lost for ever. Participating preference or preferred ordinary shareholders receive their share of any surplus distributed profits after the preference and ordinary share dividends have been paid.

If the company goes into liquidation, the accumulated arrears of preference dividends are payable after the creditors are paid off.

Ordinary shareholders are then entitled to the return of capital, in proportion to the nominal value of their shares, unless the Memorandum and Articles give the preference shareholders priority to capital. Surplus assets are usually split between ordinary and participating preference shareholders.

Redeemable preference shares are similar to debentures (see page 48) and advice should be sought before issue.

Share warrants are usually issued only to holders of fully paid-up shares but they can be attached to, for instance, a debenture issue, with the option to convert them into fully paid-up shares at a future date. They usually pay dividends when the coupon attached to the warrant is sent to the company. Unlike share certificates, however, they are negotiable, so if they are lost or stolen the original holder may have no rights against the company. Sometimes voting rights are attached but the Articles may only permit a vote on deposit of the warrant. Companies usually contact holders by newspaper advertisement only, so they often miss meetings and may not receive dividends promptly.

THE SHARE PREMIUM ACCOUNT

If you are trading profitably and have built up reserves, the true value of shares is increased. If new shares are issued at more than the par (nominal) value of previously issued shares of the same class, the premium must be transferred to a share premium account, which becomes part of the company's capital. This cannot then be distributed without the consent of the court, unless it is used for a bonus or rights issue, or to provide a premium for the redemption of redeemable preference shares or debentures. However, it can be used to write off the expenses of another issue.

REDUCING THE COMPANY'S CAPITAL

A provision in Table A (see page 20) permits you to reduce the company's capital by buying back its shares. This will be easier when the Company Law Reform Act comes into force. The current procedure is complicated, there are tax implications and the penalties for non-compliance include imprisonment and/or a fine, so you should take legal and financial advice before taking action.

COMPANY BORROWINGS: MORTGAGES, CHARGES AND DEBENTURES

Borrowing

A trading company can borrow and give security without a specific provision in its Memorandum and Articles. However, you should ensure that your company has the widest possible borrowing and investment powers to avoid problems with lenders and shareholders and specifically exclude the provisions of Table A which restrict the borrowing power of both the company and the directors.

Mortgages

A money-lending company can lodge its own shares as security in a transaction entered into by the company in the ordinary course of its business. Also, any company can mortgage partly paid-up shares for the balance remaining unpaid.

Debentures

You can raise additional capital by a debenture issue. The debenture itself is a document given by the company to the debenture holder as evidence of a mortgage or charge on company assets for a loan with interest. The holder is a creditor of the company, but often holds one of a series of debentures with similar rights attached to them or is one of a class of debenture holders whose security is transferable (like shares) or negotiable (like warrants).

Fixed charges and floating charges

If the debenture is secured by specific assets, the charge is fixed. A charge over all the company's assets – which will include stock in trade, goodwill and so on – is a floating charge, as the security changes from time to time. A floating charge, which allows the company freely to deal with business assets, automatically crystallises into a fixed charge if the company is wound up or stops trading, or if it is in default under the terms of the loan and the debenture holder takes steps to enforce the security.

You can create separate fixed and floating charges. The floating charge is always enforceable after a fixed charge, in whatever order they were made, unless it prohibits a loan with prior rights on the security of the fixed assets and the lender under the fixed charge knows of the restriction. Banks usually include this provision in their lending agreements covering the company's overdraft, so that you may have difficulties if you run into a basic liquidity problem, as cheques paid into the account after a company ceases trading may be fraudulent preferences (see page 147).

REGISTRATION OF CHARGES

All charges, which include mortgages, created by the company must be registered with the Registrar within 21 days of creation. The fee on registration is £13 and £50 for same-day registration. Your bank's charge on credit balances is not registrable unless it is charged to a third party.

If the company charges property, or the charge is created, outside the UK, the 21-day deadline can be extended by application to the Registrar before the filing deadline. The extension runs from the date when the instrument creating the charge could have been received in the UK in the normal course of business.

The requirement covers charges made as security for debentures, floating charges on the company's assets including a charge on book debts; and charges on any interest in land or goods (except, in the case of goods, where the lender is entitled to possession of the goods or of a document of title to them). It also covers charges on intangible moveable property (in Scotland, incorporeal moveable property) such as goodwill, intellectual property, book debts and uncalled share capital or calls made but not paid. Form 395 (see page 51) is used in registering a mortgage or charge and Form 397 (see page 53) for an issue of secured debentures. Unless registered, the charge is void as against the liquidator and any creditor so far as any security on the company's assets is conferred under the charge and the moneys secured are imme-diately repayable. If the company does not register the charge, the lender or some other interested person can do so.

If incorrect particulars are registered, the charge is void to the extent of the irregularity unless the court orders otherwise but the Registrar will allow a late amendment to the registered particulars. The company and its officers who are in default in registering the instruments are, in addition, liable to a fine of £200 a day until registration is effected. The holder of the unregistered charge is in the position of an unsecured creditor.

Unless the charge was created after the issue, a copy of the certificate of registration issued by the Registrar must be endorsed on every debenture or certificate of debenture stock issued by the company. Free certified copies can be obtained from Companies House.

Copies of every instrument creating a charge which requires registra-tion must be kept at the registered office but it is only necessary to provide a copy of one of a series of uniform debentures.

Charges on registered land must also be registered under the Land Registration Act 2002, and fixed charges on unregistered land regis-tered under the Land Charges Act 1972. The 2002 Act came into force in October 2003 and you should check with the Land Registry as to requirements.

When a registered charge is repaid or satisfied, a 'memorandum of satisfaction' on Form 403b (see page 191) should be filed with the Registrar.

THE CONSUMER CREDIT ACT 1974

Loans for up to £25,000 including the cost of the credit, where the company is a joint debtor with an individual, must comply with the terms of the Consumer Credit Act 1974. A joint and several obligation by the company and an individual is outside the ambit of the Act.

M

CHWP000

Please do not write in this margin

Please complete legibly, preferably in black type, or bold block lettering

* insert full name of Company

COMPANIES FORM No. 395

Particulars of a mortgage or charge

A fee of £13 is payable to Companies House in respect of each register entry for a mortgage or charge.

Pursuant to section 395 of the Companies Act 1985

395

To the Registrar of Companies
(Address overleaf - Note 6)

For official use | Company number

Name of company

*

Date of creation of the charge

Description of the instrument (if any) creating or evidencing the charge (note 2)

Amount secured by the mortgage or charge

Names and addresses of the mortgagees or persons entitled to the charge

Postcode

Presenter's name address and reference (if any) :

For official Use (02/06)
Mortgage Section

Post room

Time critical reference

Page 1

Figure 3.1 Particulars of a charge

Short particulars of all the property mortgaged or charged

Please do not write in this margin

Please complete legibly, preferably in black type, or bold block lettering

Particulars as to commission allowance or discount (note 3)

A fee is payable to Companies House in respect of each register entry for a mortgage or charge. (See Note 5)

Signed   Date

On behalf of [company][mortgagee/chargee]†

† delete as appropriate

Notes

1   The original instrument (if any) creating or evidencing the charge, together with these prescribed particulars correctly completed must be delivered to the Registrar of Companies within 21 days after the date of creation of the charge (section 395). If the property is situated and the charge was created outside the United Kingdom delivery to the Registrar must be effected within 21 days after the date on which the instrument could in due course of post, and if dispatched with due diligence, have been received in the United Kingdom (section 398). A copy of the instrument creating the charge will be accepted where the property charged is situated and the charge was created outside the United Kingdom (section 398) and in such cases the copy must be verified to be a correct copy either by the company or by the person who has delivered or sent the copy to the registrar. The verification must be signed by or on behalf of the person giving the verification and where this is given by a body corporate it must be signed by an officer of that body. A verified copy will also be accepted where section 398(4) applies (property situate in Scotland or Northern Ireland) and Form No. 398 is submitted.

2   A description of the instrument, eg "Trust Deed", "Debenture", "Mortgage", or "Legal charge", etc, as the case may be, should be given.

3   In this section there should be inserted the amount or rate per cent. of the commission, allowance or discount (if any) paid or made either directly or indirectly by the company to any person in consideration of his:
      (a) subscribing or agreeing to subscribe, whether absolutely or conditionally, or
      (b) procuring or agreeing to procure subscriptions, whether absolute or conditional,
   for any of the debentures included in this return. The rate of interest payable under the terms of the debentures should not be entered.

4   If any of the spaces in this form provide insufficient space the particulars must be entered on the prescribed continuation sheet.

5   A fee of £13 is payable to Companies House in respect of each register entry for a mortgage or charge. Cheques and Postal Orders are to be made payable to **Companies House**.

6   The address of the Registrar of Companies is: Companies House, Crown Way, Cardiff CF14 3UZ

Page 2

Figure 3.1   *continued*

COMPANIES FORM No. 397

Particulars for the registration of a charge to secure a series of debentures

397

CHFP000

A fee of £13 is payable to Companies House in respect of each register entry for a mortgage or charge.

Please do not write in this margin

Please complete legibly, preferably in black type, or bold block lettering

Pursuant to section 397 of the Companies Act 1985

To the Registrar of Companies (Address overleaf - Note 7)

For official use

Company number

Name of company

* insert full name of Company

*

Date of the covering deed (if any) (note 2) _____

Total amount secured by the whole series _____

Date of present issue _____

Amount of present issue (if any) of debentures of the series _____

Date of resolutions authorising the issue of the series _____

Names of the trustees (if any) for the debenture holders

General description of the property charged

Continue overleaf as necessary

Presenter's name address and reference (if any) :

For official Use (02/06)
Mortgage Section

Post room

Time critical reference

Page 1

Figure 3.2 Particulars for the registration of a charge to secure a series of debentures

General description of the property charged (continued)

Particulars as to commission, allowance or discount (note 3)

Signed _____ Date _____

On behalf of [company] [mortgagee / chargee]†

Notes

1 Particulars should be given on this form of a series of debentures containing (or giving by reference to any other instrument) any charge to the benefit of which the debenture holders of the series are entitled pari passu. This form is to be used for registration of particulars of the entire series, and may also be used when an issue of debentures is made at the same time as the series of debentures is created. All issues of debentures made after the registration of the series with the Registrar of Companies should be notified to the Registrar on Form No. 397a.

2 The date should be given of the covering deed (if any) by which the security is created or defined.

3 In this section there should be inserted the amount or rate per cent of the commission, allowance or discount (if any) paid or made either directly or indirectly by the company to any person in consideration of his
(a) subscribing or agreeing to subscribe, whether absolutely or conditionally, or
(b) procuring or agreeing to procure subscriptions, whether absolute or conditional,
for any of the debentures included in this return. The rate of interest payable under the terms of the debentures should not be entered.

4 The deed (if any) containing the charge must be delivered with these particulars correctly completed, to the Registrar within 21 days after it's execution. If there is no such deed, one of the debentures must be so delivered within 21 days after the execution of any debenture of the series.

5 If the spaces in this form are insufficient, the particulars may be continued on a separate sheet.

6 A fee of £13 is payable to Companies House in respect of each register entry for a mortgage or charge. Cheques and Postal Orders are to be made payable to **Companies House**.

7 The address of the Registrar of Companies is: Mortgage Section, PO Box 716, Companies House Crown Way, Cardiff CF14 3YA

Page 2

Figure 3.2 *continued*

M

CHWP000

COMPANIES FORM No. 398

**Certificate of registration in
Scotland or Northern Ireland
of a charge comprising property
situate there**

Pursuant to section 398(4) of the Companies Act 1985

398

Please do not
write in
this margin

*Please complete
legibly, preferably
in black type, or
bold block lettering*

To the Registrar of Companies
(Address overleaf)

Name of company

For official use   Company number

* insert full name
of company

*

I

of

* give date and
parties to charge

certify that the charge *

of which a true copy is annexed to this form was presented for registration on

† delete as
appropriate

in [Scotland] [Northern Ireland] †

Signed   Date

Presenter's name address and
reference (if any) :

For official Use (02/06)
Mortgage Section   Post room

Figure 3.3   Certificate of registration in Scotland or Northern Ireland
of a charge comprising property situated there

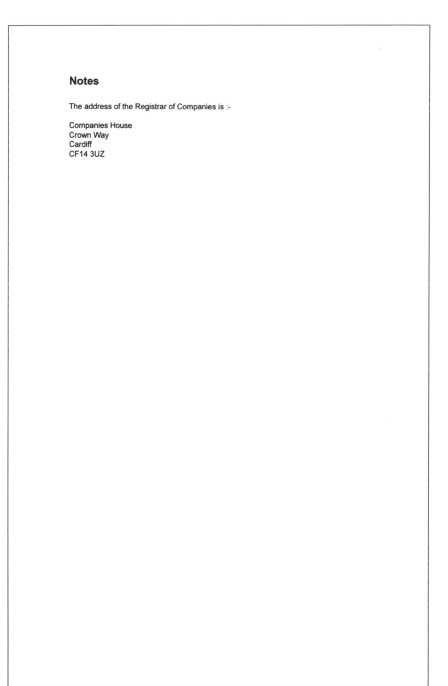

Notes

The address of the Registrar of Companies is :-

Companies House
Crown Way
Cardiff
CF14 3UZ

Figure 3.3 *continued*

COMPANIES FORM No. 400

Particulars of a mortgage or charge subject to which property has been acquired

400

CHWP000

A fee of £13 is payable to Companies House in respect of each register entry for a mortgage or charge.

Please do not write in this margin

Please complete legibly, preferably in black type, or bold block lettering

* insert full name of Company

Pursuant to section 400 of the Companies Act 1985

To the Registrar of Companies
(Address overleaf - Note 4)

For official use

Company number

Name of company

*

Date and description of the instrument (if any) creating or evidencing the mortgage or charge (note 1)

Amount secured by the mortgage or charge _____

Names and addresses of the mortgagees or persons entitled to the mortgage or charge

Short particulars of the property mortgaged or charged

Continue overleaf as necessary

Presenter's name address and reference (if any) :

For official Use (02/06)
Mortgage Section

Post room

Time critical reference

Page 1

Figure 3.4 Particulars of a mortgage or charge subject to which property has been acquired

Short particulars of the property mortgaged or charged (continued)

Date of the acquisition of the property _____

Signed _____ Designation ‡_____ Date _____

Notes

1 A description of the instrument, eg, "Trust Deed", "Debenture", etc, as the case may be, should be given.

2 A verified copy of the instrument must be delivered with these particulars correctly completed to the Registrar of Companies within 21 days after the date of the completion of the acquisition of the property which is subject to the charge. The copy must be verified to be a correct copy either by the company or by the person who has delivered or sent the copy to the registrar. The verification must be signed by or on behalf of the person giving the verification and where this is given by a body corporate it must be signed by an officer of that body. If the property is situated and the charge was created outside Great Britain, they must be delivered within 21 days after the date on which the copy of the instrument could in due course of post, and if despatched with due diligence have been received in the United Kingdom.

3 A fee of £13 is payable to Companies House in respect of each register entry for a mortgage or charge.

Cheques and Postal Orders are to be made payable to **Companies House**.

4 The address of the Registrar of Companies is:-

Companies House
Crown Way
Cardiff
CF14 3UZ

Figure 3.4 *continued*

COMPANIES FORM No. 410(Scot)

M

Particulars of a charge created
by a company registered in Scotland

CHWP000

A fee of £13 is payable to Companies House in respect
of each register entry for a mortgage or charge

410

Please do not
write in
this margin

Pursuant to section 410 of the Companies Act 1985

Please complete
legibly, preferably
in black type, or
bold block lettering

To the Registrar of Companies
(Address overleaf - Note 6)

For official use

Company number

Name of company

* insert full name
of company

*

Date of creation of the charge (note 1)

Description of the instrument (if any) creating or evidencing the charge (note 1)

Amount secured by the charge

If there is not enough
space on this form
you may use the
prescribed
continuation sheet
410cs

Names and addresses of the persons entitled to the charge

Presenter's name address telephone
number and reference (if any):

For official use (02/06)

Charges Section

Post room

Page 1

Figure 3.5 Particulars of a charge created by a company registered in Scotland

Short particulars of all the property charged.

Statement, in the case of a floating charge, as to any restrictions on power to grant further securities and any ranking provision (note 2)

Particulars as to commission, allowance or discount paid (see section 413(3))

Signed _____ Date _____

On behalf of [company] [chargee]†

Notes

1. A description of the instrument e.g. "Standard Security" "Floating Charge" etc, should be given. For the date of creation of a charge see section 410(5) of the Act. (Examples - date of signing of an Instrument of Charge; date of recording / registration of a Standard Security; date of intimation of an Assignation.)

2. In the case of a floating charge a statement should be given of (1) the restrictions, if any, on the power of the company to grant further securities ranking in priority to, or pari passu with the floating charge; and / or (2) the provisions, if any, regulating the order in which the floating charge shall rank with any other subsisting or future floating charges or fixed securities over the property which is the subject of the floating charge or any part of it.

3. A certified copy of the instrument, if any, creating or evidencing the charge, together with this form with the prescribed particulars correctly completed must be delivered to the Registrar of Companies within 21 days after the date of the creation of the charge. In the case of a charge created out of the United Kingdom comprising property situated outside the U.K., within 21 days after the date on which the copy of the instrument creating it could, in due course of post, and if despatched with due diligence, have been received in the U.K. Certified copies of any other documents relevant to the charge should also be delivered.

4. A certified copy must be signed by or on behalf of the person giving the certification and where this is a body corporate it must be signed by an officer of that body.

5. A fee of £13 is payable to Companies House in respect of each register entry for a mortgage or charge. Cheques and Postal Orders are to be made payable to **Companies House**.

6. The address of the Registrar of Companies is: Companies House, 37 Castle Terrace, Edinburgh EH1 2EB
   DX 235 Edinburgh   or   LP - 4 Edinburgh 2

Page 2

Figure 3.5 *continued*

www.GetFactoring.com

UK Freephone Number 0800 328 9784

Business Gateways Ltd

Is your business looking for improved cash flow to grow?

Are you trading business to business?

Do you offer credit terms to your customers?

Then FACTORING could be your answer

Factoring provides the finance to improve your cash flow by releasing money tied-up in trade debtors giving you the working capital to grow your business.

How does it work?
Basically the principle is simple – as invoices are raised the factoring company will advance you up to an agreed percentage of the value of the invoice – can be as high as 85%.

Want to know more?
GetFactoring offers a factoring consultancy service free-of-charge and is able to give you advice as to whether factoring or invoice discounting will be beneficial to your business. We can explain how it works and what it costs and help you source a suitable facility.

If you want to know more please visit our website
www.getfactoring.com
Or email us at **advice@getfactoring.com**
Alternatively call us on our UK freephone number **0800 328 9784**

Stuck?

Get your business past 'GO' with our innovative factoring solutions.

Our factoring solutions can release the capital you need to get your business moving.

Call us today - **0870 243 1836**
or visit www.charterhousefactoring.com

Oakfield House, 35 Perrymount Road,
Haywards Heath, West Sussex, RH16 3BW

Tel: 0870 243 1836

Fax: 0870 243 1837

email: sales@charterhousefactoring.com

Registered in England & Wales Registered No. 05106936
©2005 All Rights Reserved. 9076(7031)0606

CHARTERHOUSE COMMERCIAL FINANCE PLC
a member of
CHARTERHOUSE GROUP INTERNATIONAL

4

Directors

The private limited company must have at least one director, although he or she cannot also be the secretary. Your Articles can specify the maximum number of directors.

WHO IS A DIRECTOR?

Anyone, with whatever title and however appointed, who acts as a director, is regarded as a director.

WHO CAN BE A DIRECTOR?

Anyone can be appointed as director unless disqualified by the Articles except for:

- an undischarged bankrupt, unless his or her appointment is approved by the court;
- someone disqualified by court order;
- the company's auditor.

Your Articles usually disqualify anyone who is of unsound mind or who is absent from board meetings for more than six months without consent. A company can be your corporate director, and directors need not hold shares unless this is required by the Articles.

There is no minimum or maximum age limit but:

▦ a child must be able to sign the consent to act;
▦ you should take legal advice if the child is very young;
▦ the Registrar in Scotland will not register a director under 16; and
▦ some non-British citizens are excluded – so check for clearance with the Home Office Immigration and Nationality Directorate, Lunar House, Wellesley Road, Croydon CR9 2BY (tel: 0845 010 5200) or check the website, www.ind.homeoffice.gov.uk.

APPOINTMENT OF DIRECTORS

The first directors can be appointed:

▦ by the subscribers to the Memorandum (who must sign the Notice of Appointment filed on incorporation) unless the Articles permit a majority to act;
▦ by naming them in the Articles, when the appointment takes effect from the date of incorporation;
▦ by appointment at the first company meeting;
▦ by appointment under a specific provision in the Articles.

Additional and subsequent appointments are made in accordance with the Articles and you can provide for appointment by shareholders in proportion to their holdings. The usual provision permits appointment by the board to fill vacancies, or to appoint additional directors subject to a specified maximum. The new director must then retire at the Annual General Meeting following appointment, immediately standing for re-election. Unless the Articles provide otherwise, the shareholders must have 28 days' notice of the proposal.

Details of the appointment of directors must be filed on Form 288a, signed by the officer confirming his or her consent to act but the appointment is effective even if the notice is not filed. The resignation or retirement of directors or the secretary and changes in their particulars, however, must be filed with the Registrar on Forms 288a, 288b and 288c respectively (see pages 67–69).

RETIREMENT AND REMOVAL

Usually, a third of the directors retire by rotation each year, standing for re-election at the Annual General Meeting unless the Articles otherwise provide. They are technically out of office until re-elected by the shareholders.

Removal is by a majority vote of the shareholders and the shareholders and the director must have 28 days' notice of the proposal.

The board of directors

Only a sole director can make his or her own decisions. If there are two or more directors they must work through the board which usually conducts and controls company business. Formal meetings are, however, often dispensed with and the board can delegate its powers to one or more board members and appoint a managing director.

Part-time directors. Non-executive directors with financial, legal or technical expertise can be appointed.

Alternate directors who speak and act on behalf of board members in their temporary absence can be appointed if you have an appropriate provision in the Articles.

Nominee directors are appointed to represent substantial shareholders. They must not act solely in their principal's interests but, like any other director, in the interests of the company as a whole.

Shadow directors are persons in accordance with whose instructions the directors are accustomed to act and they have the same duties and obligations as any other directors. Your professional advisers, however, are not regarded as shadow directors.

DIRECTORS AS EMPLOYEES

Directors are company employees. They have no right under the Articles to remuneration, notice or compensation for loss of office but they have the same rights as other employees under the employment legislation provided they receive a salary. They should therefore be employed under a service contract setting out their terms and conditions of employment, including pension arrangements, the level of contributions to be paid for life assurance and details of benefits in kind.

Contracts exceeding five years must be approved by the company in general meeting and must be available for inspection at the company's registered office or principal place of business. If there is no full written contract, a written memorandum or note of the terms of employment must be included and details of the place of inspection must be sent to the Registrar.

DIRECTORS' DUTIES

A director is a constitutional monarch bound by the terms of the company's charter set out in the Memorandum and Articles. He or she can exercise all the powers permitted by them which are not reserved to be exercised by the shareholders in general meeting. If he or she is the majority shareholder and sole director, his or her rule may be despotic.

He or she must, however, act in accordance with the Companies Acts and the general law and has three primary duties:

- a fiduciary duty to the company to act honestly and in good faith in the best interests of the company as a whole;
- a duty to exercise such a degree of skill and care in carrying out his or her duties as might reasonably be expected from someone of his or her ability and experience;
- a duty to carry out the statutory obligations imposed by the Companies Acts and other legislation.

FIDUCIARY DUTY

Directors in position of trust

This is the duty to act honestly, in good faith and in the best interests of the company. It imposes a trustee's responsibility on directors to take proper care of the assets and to ensure payments are properly made and supported by adequate documentation. Directors must not make a personal profit at the company's expense and must disclose to the other directors at board meetings any interest in company transactions. Disclosure should also be made at general meetings and it should be formally minuted.

Companies House — for the record —

Please complete in typescript, or in bold black capitals.

CHWP000

288a

APPOINTMENT of director or secretary

(NOT for resignation (use Form 288b) or change of particulars (use Form 288c))

Company Number

Company Name in full

	Day	Month	Year		Day	Month	Year
Date of appointment				†Date of Birth			

Appointment form

Notes on completion appear on reverse.

Appointment as director | | as secretary | | Please mark the appropriate box. If appointment is as a director and secretary mark both boxes.

NAME *Style / Title | *Honours etc

Forename(s)

Surname

Previous Forename(s) | Previous Surname(s)

†† Tick this box if the address shown is a service address for the beneficiary of a Confidentiality Order granted under the provisions of section 723B of the Companies Act 1985

†† **Usual residential address**

Post town | Postcode

County / Region | Country

†Nationality | †Business occupation

†Other directorships (additional space overleaf)

Consent signature

I consent to act as ** director / secretary of the above named company

Date

* Voluntary details.
† Directors only.
**Delete as appropriate

A director, secretary etc must sign the form below.

Signed | Date

(**a director / secretary / administrator / administrative receiver / receiver manager / receiver)

You do not have to give any contact information in the box opposite but if you do, it will help Companies House to contact you if there is a query on the form. The contact information that you give will be visible to searchers of the public record..

Tel

DX number | DX exchange

Companies House receipt date barcode

This form has been provided free of charge by Companies House

Form 10/03

When you have completed and signed the form please send it to the Registrar of Companies at:

Companies House, Crown Way, Cardiff, CF14 3UZ   DX 33050 Cardiff
for companies registered in England and Wales   or
Companies House, 37 Castle Terrace, Edinburgh, EH1 2EB
for companies registered in Scotland   DX 235 Edinburgh
                                                    or LP - 4 Edinburgh 2

Figure 4.1   Appointment of a director or secretary

Companies House
— for the record —

288b

Please complete in typescript, or in bold black capitals.

CHWP000

Terminating appointment as director or secretary
(NOT for appointment (use Form 288a) or change of particulars (use Form 288c))

Company Number

Company Name in full

Date of termination of appointment

Day Month Year

as director   as secretary

Please mark the appropriate box. If terminating appointment as a director and secretary mark both boxes.

NAME — *Style / Title

Please insert details as previously notified to Companies House.

Forename(s)

Surname

*Honours etc

†Date of Birth

Day Month Year

A serving director, secretary etc must sign the form below.

Signed   **Date**

* Voluntary details.
† Directors only.
** Delete as appropriate

(** serving director / secretary / administrator / administrative receiver / receiver manager / receiver)

You do not have to give any contact information in the box opposite but if you do, it will help Companies House to contact you if there is a query on the form. The contact information that you give will be visible to searchers of the public record.

Tel

DX number   DX exchange

Companies House receipt date barcode

This form has been provided free of charge by Companies House.

When you have completed and signed the form please send it to the Registrar of Companies at:
Companies House, Crown Way, Cardiff, CF14 3UZ   DX 33050 Cardiff
for companies registered in England and Wales   or
Companies House, 37 Castle Terrace, Edinburgh, EH1 2EB
for companies registered in Scotland   DX 235 Edinburgh
                                                    or LP - 4 Edinburgh

Form revised 10/03

Figure 4.2 Resignation of a director or secretary

Companies House
— *for the record* —

Please complete in typescript,
or in bold black capitals.

CHWP000

288c
CHANGE OF PARTICULARS for director
or secretary *(NOT for appointment (use Form 288a) or resignation (use Form 288b))*

Company Number

Company Name in full

		Day	Month	Year

Changes of particulars form

Complete in all cases

Date of change of particulars

Name *Style / Title*   *Honours etc

Forename(s)

Surname

	Day	Month	Year

† Date of Birth

Change of name *(enter new name)* Forename(s)

Surname

Change of usual residential address ††

(enter new address)

†† **Tick this box if the address shown is a service address for the beneficiary of a Confidentiality Order granted under the provisions of section 723B of the Companies Act 1985**

Post town

County / Region   Postcode

Country

Other change
(please specify)

A serving director, secretary etc must sign the form below.

* Voluntary details.
† Directors only.
**Delete as appropriate.

Signed   **Date**

(** director / secretary / administrator / administrative receiver / receiver manager / receiver)

You do not have to give any contact information in the box opposite but if you do, it will help Companies House to contact you if there is a query on the form. The contact information that you give will be visible to searchers of the public record..

Tel

DX number   DX exchange

Companies House receipt date barcode

This form has been provided free of charge by Companies House

Form 10/03

When you have completed and signed the form please send it to the Registrar of Companies at:
Companies House, Crown Way, Cardiff, CF14 3UZ   DX 33050 Cardiff
for companies registered in England and Wales   or
Companies House, 37 Castle Terrace, Edinburgh, EH1 2EB
for companies registered in Scotland   DX 235 Edinburgh
                                            or LP - 4 Edinburgh 2

Figure 4.3   Change of particulars for a director or secretary

The directors' personal interests must not conflict with those of the company and they must not use its assets, including knowledge acquired through the company, for personal benefit.

DIRECTORS AS AGENTS

Because the company is a separate legal entity, a director can only act as the company's agent, acting on his or hr principal's (the company's) instructions, express or implied. For instance, a director's signature on a company contract binds the company but if he or she signs contracts in his or her own name, without any reference to the company, he or she can be personally liable under the contract.

COMPANY CONTRACTS

Interest in contracts

Directors' personal interests and the interests of persons connected with them (see page 72), direct or indirect, in company contracts must be disclosed. Disclosure must be to the board, and the director cannot thereafter take part in discussing the transaction. If the interested director votes on the contract, the transaction can be set aside by the company. In some circumstances details must also be shown in the audited accounts (see page 73).

BORROWING FROM THE COMPANY

Loans to directors, connected persons and employees

Companies can:

- make loans;
- extend guarantees;
- provide security in connection with loans to directors, shadow directors and anyone connected with them to a maximum of

£10,000, if made on the same basis as would apply to someone of the same financial standing as the borrower.

Also permitted are:

- Short-term (for two months) quasi-loans of up to £5,000, if repayable within two months. For this purpose, a quasi-loan is an undertaking by the company to reimburse the borrower's creditor.
- Loans of up to £10,000 if made in the ordinary course of business and on the same basis as would apply to someone of the same financial standing as the borrower.
- Loans of up to £20,000 to enable a director to meet properly incurred business expenses. The transaction must be approved in advance by the shareholders in a general meeting or made on condition that, if not approved at the next Annual General Meeting, the company will be reimbursed within six months of the meeting.
- Unlimited loans if made in the ordinary course of business and available on the same terms to outsiders.

MONEY-LENDING COMPANIES

Money-lending companies that ordinarily provide such loans to employees can lend directors up to £100,000 to buy, or pay for, improvements to their only or main residence for tax purposes. This is, however, a maximum from which any other cash or credit facilities already extended to them must be deducted.

There is no limit on loans made by money-lending companies and their 'connections' in the ordinary course of business if they might properly have been made on the same terms to an outsider.

Money-lending companies can also make loans or quasi-loans and extend guarantees to directors and their 'connections', provided the company would give similar facilities to outsiders in the ordinary course of business. For this purpose, a quasi-loan is an undertaking by the company to reimburse a creditor of the director or connected person.

CONNECTED PERSONS

Persons 'connected with' a director broadly comprise the director's partner, spouse, child and step-child. They also include a company with which the director is associated and of which he or she controls at least one-fifth of the votes at general meetings, a trustee of any trust under which the director, the family group or the associated companies are beneficiaries, and the partner of a 'connected' person.

LOANS TO EMPLOYEES

There is no top limit on an advance made to set up a trust to buy shares in the company for employees, including full-time salaried directors, or on the amount employees may borrow to buy company shares. The company can, however, assist anyone in the purchase of its shares, provided that the company's assets are not thereby reduced or, to the extent of the reduction, the finance comes out of distributable profits.

The assistance can be by gift, loan guarantee, security, indemnity or any other financial help which materially reduces the net assets.

The smaller business has some tax concessions here but the statutory provisions are complicated and you should seek expert advice before calling on your company's generosity.

THE CONSUMER CREDIT ACT 1974

Transactions of under £25,000, including the cost of the credit, must comply with the terms of the Consumer Credit Act 1974.

USE OF COMPANY ASSETS

Private use of company assets is restricted. Non-cash assets valued at £2,000, or at 10 per cent of the company's paid-up share capital, cannot be acquired by the company or handed over to directors or connected persons without the prior approval of the shareholders in general meeting. Approval can be retrospective if given within a reasonable period of the transaction. If annual accounts have been prepared in accordance with the Companies Acts, the limit goes up to £100,000 or a maximum of 10 per cent of the company's net assets as stated in the most recent accounts.

DISCLOSURE

Credit facilities, agreements to arrange credit, and the provision of guarantees and security to directors and connected persons must be disclosed in the annual accounts or the directors' report, unless the company's contingent net liability during the period covered by the accounts does not exceed £10,000. Any other transactions or arrangements between the directors and connected persons must also be included in the accounts, unless the net value does not exceed £12,000 or 1 per cent of the net value of the company's assets to a maximum of £10,000.

FINES AND PENALTIES

Credit facilities extended in contravention of the legislation and ultra vires transactions can be cancelled by the company. The company is entitled to reimbursement unless this is impossible, or the company has been indemnified for loss and damage, or an outsider without knowledge of the contravention might suffer loss. If restitution is not possible, the contravenor and any director authorising the transaction are liable to reimburse or indemnify the company. In addition, they have to recompense it for any consequential gain or loss unless they can prove they did not know the transaction was unlawful. If the transaction is with a director's connection, the connected director is not liable if he or she took all reasonable steps to ensure that the company complied with the Companies Acts.

There is no way to save an unlawful transfer of assets by providing an indemnity through a third party.

SHARE DEALINGS

There is no restriction on directors' share and debenture dealings, as long as the company is kept informed and details entered on the company's Register of Directors' Interests.

SKILL AND CARE

Directors must exercise the degree of skill and care that may reasonably be expected from someone in their position with their ability and experience. Professionally qualified directors must therefore act with the care and diligence expected from a member of their profession and, unless they are part-time directors, should devote themselves full time to the job.

Non-executive directors are usually not involved in day-to-day management and the only requirement is that they regularly attend board meetings. They must exercise an independent standard of judgement and if they are properly to fulfil the purpose of their appointment they should be encouraged to participate fully in board decisions.

DELEGATION

The directors can delegate their duties but they must be satisfied that they are delegating to a suitable person who is competent, reliable and honest. They cannot simply abandon responsibility but must keep themselves informed as to progress.

STATUTORY DUTIES

The directors' *administrative duties* are contained mainly in the Companies Acts and the Insolvency Act 1986.

Both the company and its officers can be fined for failure to comply with the statutory requirements, and persistent default can lead to disqualification from acting as a director or from being involved in company management for up to 15 years, or imprisonment. Fines, payable on demand, apply to the late filing of accounts. They range from £100 for accounts delivered up to three months late to £1,000 for a delay of over 12 months and are in addition to fines imposed on the directors in the criminal courts. The criminal penalties for failure to deliver the accounts or the annual return and failure to notify a change of directors or company secretary are set out in Appendix 3. Directors of small companies therefore often pass these duties to their accountants or solicitors (who are experienced in company administration) so that they can concentrate on management. This is an appropriate delegation of duty but the directors are still required to supervise and they are ultimately responsible for ensuring that the company complies with legal requirements.

The *statutory books* and the *annual return* are dealt with on pages 89 and 92. Although the company secretary is responsible for maintaining the statutory books, the directors' duty to supervise requires that they ensure the company keeps proper records and files the necessary documentation with the Registrar in compliance with the statutory requirements.

DIRECTORS' LIABILITY

Limited liability means that the company is responsible for business debts and obligations. Liabilities can, however, be passed to directors and management but only in specific circumstances.

The directors have unlimited powers to bind the company, whatever the restrictions imposed by the Memorandum, the Articles or the shareholders, provided the person with whom they are dealing is acting in good faith. However, the company can repudiate an *ultra vires* transaction entered into by a director, a connected person or the board. The directors or the board may then be liable to the company but a connected person is only liable if he or she knew that the directors were exceeding their powers.

The directors are liable personally for breach of statutory or other duty or where there is fraud but they are only liable for negligence if they are clearly at fault.

Directors may also be liable personally if they, or the company, to their knowledge act outside the powers given by the Memorandum and Articles or if they contract without reference to the company by, for instance, placing orders without stating that they are acting on behalf of the company. They are also liable on cheques and other negotiable instruments which do not carry the company's full registered name.

Directors are liable for 'misfeasance' (wrongdoing): for instance, making secret profits at the company's expense. 'Nonfeasance' (doing nothing), however, may bring no liability unless it comes within the matters to be considered on an application for disqualification. A director can apply to the court for relief in any proceedings for negligence, default, breach of duty or trust and the court will relieve him or her of liability if satisfied that he or she acted reasonably and honestly and, in the circumstances, ought fairly to be excused.

EMPLOYERS' DUTIES

The legal obligations imposed on employers relating to employees and third parties affected by the company's business activities apply to all employers. Because of the protection of limited liability, claims are made against the company. Although the directors are responsible for ensuring compliance with the law, liability is only passed to them if there is fraud or, in some circumstances, negligence.

THE DIRECTORS, THE COMPANY AND THE SHAREHOLDERS

Minority shareholders have no say in the running of the business and if management is inefficient a shareholder may be able to do nothing. It is only the company itself – that is, the majority shareholders – who can take action. Provided directors act in good faith and in the interests of the company as a whole, the majority shareholders can do anything permitted by the Memorandum and Articles and can ratify almost any transaction, even retrospectively, in general meeting.

A single shareholder can, however, sue the company in his or her own name to protect his or her individual rights, for example to compel the board to accept his or her vote at general meetings, or if there is unfair prejudice, fraud or 'gross negligence'. A group of 10 per cent of the shareholders can call in the Department of Trade and Industry to investigate the company and in some circumstances the court can take action against management. The directors may then lose the protection of limited liability and be ordered to compensate the company or the shareholder for loss.

DIRECTORS AND OUTSIDERS

Third party claims on directors are usually made by unpaid creditors when the company goes into insolvent liquidation and the protection of limited liability is lost if there has been fraudulent or wrongful trading. Liability can fall on non-executive shadow and nominee directors, as well as full-time working directors.

Fraudulent trading is trading with intent to defraud creditors. It can arise when cheques are paid into the company's bank account after a company stops trading, even if paid in under the genuine and reasonable belief that creditors will be paid in a short time. Floating charges and loans are invalid if made within six months of a winding up, unless the company was solvent when the loan was made; in some circumstances the directors must repay the creditor and may also be liable to prosecution.

Wrongful trading. Penalties here extend to disqualification and imprisonment but only if it is proved that at some time before the liquidation the company was trading although the director knew, or ought to have known, that there was no reasonable prospect that it could avoid insolvent liquidation.

For 12 months after insolvent liquidation the directors and shadow directors cannot act for a company with the same name. The court's consent is required before they act for a company using its former name or trading name or one suggesting a continuing association with it.

Personal guarantees are a problem only when the company cannot pay its debts. A guarantee on the bank overdraft is probably the most usual undertaking required from directors in support of a company. This is often backed up by a charge on a director's home. The bank usually requires the director's spouse to be a joint and several guarantor to give the bank priority to the spouse's claim to the equity in the property. A director is advised to resist a request for a charge on personal assets, particularly on his or her home, as a charge given for business purposes removes the protection under the general law given to residential owners. Independent legal advice should be sought before any guarantees are given.

BUSINESS LEASES

Landlords often require directors to join in a lease of company premises as surety. If the company cannot pay rent, the landlord can then turn to the directors for payment and they remain liable until the lease expires, even if the lease is assigned or the landlord consents to their release.

Business Insurance

Get a little help from the UK's leading specialist.

When you're starting a new business, insurance is just one of the things you're expected to be an instant expert on.

Premierline Direct is the UK's leading direct business insurance specialist and over 250,000 small businesses have come to us for help with their insurance. We'll use all of our experience to tailor a policy around the specific needs of your business - which means you get a competitively priced premium, with no compromise on the level of cover you receive.

We make it easy too. Rather than send you lots of complicated forms to fill in, we'll take the details of your business, provide a quote and even give you immediate cover. All with one phone call!

And we know that every penny counts when you're starting up. By dealing directly with us and not through a broker, we could save you hundreds of pounds. In fact, on average, our customers save over 25%* on their premiums.

To receive a quote for your business, call us today or visit us online, leave your details and we'll call you back at a time to suit you.

To help you understand just what you might need cover for, check out our at a glance guide to Business Insurance Basics.

premierline direct

✓ust business insurance

The Premierline Direct Guide to Business Insurance Basics

Public and Products Liability - Provides cover against injury to the public and damage to their property. It also includes liability arising from the sale or supply of goods or services.

Employer's Liability - Covers you for damages, legal costs and expenses if one of your employees is injured or discriminated against at work and takes out a claim.

Business Interruption Cover - If you are unable to trade following a claim, this helps to keep you in business. Cover is for the reduction in gross income and reasonable additional expenditure incurred in order to maintain business continuity.

Commercial Vehicle Insurance - If your business relies on its transport, you need insurance that helps to keep you on the road. Premierline Direct policies offer a replacement vehicle if yours is off the road for an accident repair. And covering all of your vehicles on one policy makes managing your insurance much easier.

Extensions of Cover - Provides cover for a range of situations such as damage to fixed glass and shop fronts, loss of money and damage to external blinds and signs. Many Premierline Direct policies offer automatic extensions of cover, with the option to increase limits on request.

Loss of Accounts Receivable - This provides cover for money that you are owed by customers, which cannot be collected because records have been lost or damaged by an insured risk.

Call Premierline Direct NOW for a quote

0800 058 2226

Lines open Monday - Friday 8am - 6pm and Saturday 9am - 12.30pm

www.premierlinedirect.co.uk

The terms of the lease may require companies qualifying for the audit exemption to produce audited accounts.

COMMERCIAL CONTRACTS

Finance companies often require directors to guarantee payments made by the company on instalment contracts. The contracts provide that in the event of premature termination, the full balance is immediately due and payable, and the directors are liable to pay the full amount if the company cannot do so.

INSURANCE

The company can indemnify its officers and auditors against liability for negligence, default, breach of duty and breach of trust. The cover is for both civil and criminal proceedings, provided judgement is given in their favour, they are acquitted or relief is granted by the court. You may want to arrange additional insurance to cover the unindemnifiable risk, with the party at risk paying an appropriate proportion of the premium.

The Articles must, however, include an appropriate provision giving the company the power to purchase the insurance, and details of the insurance must be included in the directors' report.

DISQUALIFICATION

Directors may be disqualified:

- on conviction for an offence connected with the promotion, formation, management or liquidation of the company;
- in a winding up, if the company continued to trade with intent to defraud creditors;
- if guilty of a fraud in relation to the company;
- for non-compliance with the Companies Acts, but there must have been 'persistent default', that is, at least three offences within five years.

Disqualification can be for up to 15 years and the court has discretion whether or not to make the order. It must, however, disqualify a director whose conduct in relation to the company, alone or together with his or her conduct as director of another company, makes him or her, in the court's opinion, unfit to be concerned in the management of a company.

The Register of Disqualification Orders, maintained by the Secretary of State, is open to public inspection. Anyone acting while disqualified is jointly and severally liable with the company employing him or her for debts incurred during the period of disqualification, and liability extends to anyone acting on their instructions.

The Companies House disqualified directors list gives details of disqualification orders for directors in England, Wales and Scotland. It is on microfiche and is updated weekly.

LubbockFine
Chartered Accountants

We work in the real world.
(where there is such a thing as a free lunch)

Lubbock Fine is an independent firm of chartered accountants working for real people right across the real world. Our multi-disciplined approach and broad perspective drives us to produce value-for-money, pragmatic solutions that really benefit our clients.

We will work with you from your business's inception and throughout its growth, adapting services as and when necessary. Drawing upon diverse experience gained from involvement across a broad range of businesses, we can work in partnership with you to develop your business to its full potential.

As a first step to a free, initial consultation, why not call **Mark Turner**, partner on **020 7490 7766** or send him an email to **markturner@lubbockfine.co.uk**

Now whoever said that there's no such thing as a free lunch?

LubbockFine
Chartered Accountants

Russell Bedford House, City Forum
250 City Road, London EC1V 2QQ
Tel: +44 (0)20 7490 7766
Fax: +44 (0)20 7490 5102
www.lubbockfine.co.uk

Registered to carry on audit work and regulated for a range of investment business
activities by the Institute of Chartered Accountants in England and Wales

ANGEL
FINANCE & PROPERTY SERVICES

YOUR ONE-STOP SHOP TO FINANCIAL FREEDOM!

DO YOU NEED HELP TO SET UP OR GROW YOUR BUSINESS?

ARE YOU A PROPERTY INVESTOR WANTING TO GROW AND MANAGE YOUR PROPERTY PORTFOLIO?

DON'T JUMP IN THE DEEPER END WITHOUT SPEAKING TO US!

We are:
- Book Keepers & Accountants
- Business Consultants
- Mortgage Brokers
- Property Sales & Lettings Agents

Our Services include:
- Company Registration, VAT, Self Assessment, Corp. Tax & Payroll
- Out-sourced Book keeping & Accounting service on a Fixed Fee basis

- Business Planning & Cash-flow Preparation for Start ups & Growing Businesses
- Business Loans & Overdrafts

- Quick Mortgage Services with minimum arrangement fee.
- Property Sales @ Fixed Fee Commission
- Property Lettings @ just 1.5 week's introductory commission

Don't get tossed about. Get your shelter under one roof!
CALL: 020 7474 4242

Angel Finance & Property Services is a trading name of Angel Investments (UK) Ltd. Registered in England No. 5620280
F32 Waterfront Studios, Royal Victoria Docks, 1 Dock Road, London E16 1AG. Tel: 020 7474 4242 Fax: 020 7474 4700.

■ Accountancy Services ■ Business Consultancy ■ Mortgage Brokers ■ Property Sales & Lettings

5

Running the company

The price of limited liability is a certain amount of publicity – documentation and reports must be sent to the Companies Registry, where some are available for public inspection on payment of a fee. In addition, you must make regular reports to shareholders and accounts must conform with the requirements of the Companies Acts.

Notices, copies of accounts and reports can be filed with Companies House by electronic means, that is, via telephone, fax, e-mail or by posting them on a website. Some forms can be downloaded from the Companies House website in PDF format and completed on-screen, then printed, signed and returned to Companies House. Information for Forms 288a, b and c (appointment, termination of appointment and change of particulars of directors or secretaries) and Form 287 (change of address of the registered office) can be submitted electronically. You must, however, use the software from a package supplier or in-house software tested with, and approved by, Companies House. Information is available from Companies House Direct help desk on 0345 573991. Forms can also be ordered to be sent to you by post.

Accounts, summary financial statements and reports can also be sent electronically to shareholders, debenture-holders and auditors. Provided that you notify the recipients, they can also be published on a website for at least 21 days before the general meeting before which they are to be laid. Announcement that notices are on a website must contain specified details about the meeting and your shareholders can send proxy forms and other notices to you via e-mail.

Accountancy…and more

Cranleys Chartered Accountants provide in-depth accountancy services but what makes us different is that we go well beyond this by offering a comprehensive range of advice, support and finance related assistance that can help a business achieve real success or significantly enhance personal wealth.

Especially suited to small and medium sized businesses (SME's) our services can help them get control of their finances, remove financial constraints, reduce liabilities and drive the business forward. Overall, we simply make it easier for owners and directors to run their businesses more efficiently.

The expertise and experience of our friendly team of professional staff includes bookkeeping, taxation, payroll, cash management, management accounts, auditing, internal audit / assurance and asset management.

Accountancy Services

Bookkeeping • Business & management accounts • PAYE/NIC • Payroll • Self-assessment tax returns • Cash management • Statutory audits • Compliance with agreements or regulations • Accounting procedures, systems and practices • Fraud prevention and investigations • Due diligence procedures • Company secretarial • Incorporation of companies

Tax & Financial Advice

Corporate tax • Personal tax • Capital gains tax • VAT • Advice on mergers and acquisitions • Innovative solutions to improve finances or prospects • Recommendations for improving cash flow and profitability • Capital restructuring and appraisals • Retirement planning to produce income streams • Tax efficient investment advice • Effective inheritance tax planning

Colin Davison, senior partner at Cranleys, is an expert on inheritance and property tax and author of two published books: 'Property Tax Secrets' and 'Inheritance Tax Secrets'.

Business Support & Development

Business valuations • Valuing goodwill • Raising capital or debt finance • Advice on sources of finance and grants • Business Plans for start-ups and existing companies • Linking business plans to operational goals

Virtual Finance Director

It is not financially viable or realistic for smaller organisations to employ a full time Finance Director. A Cranleys senior partner can act as non-executive Finance Manager or Director and the level of involvement can be as little or as much as required. This can include:

Maintaining accurate financial records • Attending Board & Management meetings • Producing budgets and forecasts • Year-end audit and draft statutory accounts • Due diligence work • Monitoring business performance • Identifying any obstacles to growth • Providing impartial, objective feedback to ideas or potential changes

Our Commitment

The following expresses our business philosophy and commitment to our clients:
- ☐ We will identify all relevant tax saving strategies
- ☐ We can be contacted daytime, evening and weekends
- ☐ We will respond to any message left within 24 hours
- ☐ We will respond to any written correspondence within seven days
- ☐ Evening and weekend appointments will always be available
- ☐ If necessary we will complete accounts within 14 days
- ☐ Tax returns will be completed within 14 days (from receipt of all necessary information
- ☐ We believe in fixed quotes for services – a client will know what fees are in advance with no surprise bills

And we will always endeavour to:
- ☐ Avoid using jargon
- ☐ Ensure you are not kept waiting for an appointment
- ☐ Keep you fully informed about what is happening with your financial affairs
- ☐ Respect confidentiality
- ☐ Complete every task on or ahead of time
- ☐ Bring new ideas to your attention that can help you succeed in achieving your goals

Free Business Health Check

To help us understand your needs, assess the expertise you might require and, importantly, formulate an effective plan to improve your wealth or business performance, we offer an initial, comprehensive business health check that's completely free of charge.

For more information about the free initial consultancy or any of our services please contact:

Colin Davison **T:** 01252 852220   **E:** colin.davison@cranleys.co.uk

Cranleys Chartered Accountants, Business Advice Centre, 24 Finns Business Park, Crondall, Farnham, Surrey GU10 5RX

www.cranleys.co.uk

Towards a better tomorrow

Whatever your accountancy requirements, Cranleys Chartered Accountants can provide the friendly and helpful service you are looking for. With offices in Hook and Fleet in Hampshire, we specialise in helping high-nett worth individuals and owner-managed businesses. Our philosophy is quite simple: work closely with clients to enhance their wealth or improve their financial stability.

Attentive and efficient, results driven accountancy service offering:

- Investment and asset management for individuals and business owners
- Taxation advice & assistance
- Specialist property tax advice for investors & developers
- Profit consulting
  - all key aspects of business processes and financial performance
- Business valuation services
- Client advisory services - comprehensive range of dedicated accountancy services
- Specialist tax service for consultants, independent directors and professional contractors

If any of our accountancy and related services is of interest we would be very pleased to discuss your requirements.

Contact:

E: colin.davison@cranleys.co.uk   T: 01256 766655   W: www.cranleys.co.uk

THE REGISTERED OFFICE

Your company must have a registered office to which formal communications and notices, including notice of legal proceedings, are sent. The address determines the tax district which deals with the company's return and tax affairs, except for PAYE, which is usually dealt with by the local collector of taxes where the wages records are kept.

The address need not be the company's main trading address and it is often convenient to use the address of the company's accountant or solicitor.

DISPLAYING THE COMPANY NAME

The company name must be fixed to, or painted on, the outside of the registered office in a prominent position, as well as at each of the company's offices, factories and places of business.

BUSINESS LETTERS AND OTHER DOCUMENTATION

The company name must appear on all business letters, cheques and other negotiable instruments, order forms, invoices and on the company seal. The letterhead must also show the registered number and registered office address but you can choose to list the names either of all directors or none of them – you cannot list a selection of named directors.

If the company is registered for VAT, invoices must in addition show the VAT registration number, the invoice number, date of supply, description of the supply, amount payable excluding VAT, the rate of VAT and the amount, the rate of any cash discount and the customer's name and address.

DIRECTORS

The appointment and removal of directors and their obligations are dealt with in Chapter 4. You may want to appoint a managing director, although he or she has no specific powers under the Companies Acts. His or her authority is based entirely on the terms and conditions of his or her service contract or those imposed by the board.

Table A (see page 20) enables the directors to delegate any of their powers to the managing director, who often looks after day-to-day management although he or she will not usually exercise the company's borrowing powers.

The chairman is the director who chairs board and general meetings. He or she can be named in the Articles, be appointed at the first directors' meeting to hold office for a specified period, or be appointed at each meeting to act as chairman. Table A gives him or her a casting vote if there is deadlock on the board and he or she has no other special powers although they can be set out in the Articles.

COMPANY SECRETARY

Under the new Company Law Reform Act you will no longer need a company secretary. Until then, however, your company must have a company secretary, who can also be a director provided he or she is not the sole director. The secretary has important duties and obligations; Table A provides that he or she be appointed by the directors for such term at such remuneration and on such conditions as they may think fit and they can also remove him or her.

The secretary is the company's chief administrative officer with ostensible authority in day-to-day administrative matters. His or her duties include the convening of board and company meetings, taking minutes of meetings, keeping the company's statutory books up to date, filing returns and forms with the Registrar and dealing with share transfers and proxies.

The first secretary must be named in the documents lodged prior to registration so his or her appointment should be minuted at the first directors' meeting.

THE STATUTORY BOOKS

The company secretary is responsible for maintaining the statutory registers and books. The statutory requirements are technical and in many smaller companies they are kept by the auditors, who also file the necessary documentation with the Registrar.

The statutory books are a useful record of the company's business activities and comprise the following:

The *Register of Members*, which lists the names and addresses of the subscribers to the Memorandum of Association and of all other shareholders, with details of their shareholdings. It must be kept at the registered office or at some other office designated by the directors. Entries can be removed after a person has ceased to hold shares for 20 years.

The *Register of Debenture Holders*, which lists similar information relating to debenture holders.

The *Register of Directors and Secretaries*, setting out the directors, full forenames and surnames and any former names, their usual residential address, nationality, business occupation and details of any other directorships held within the previous five years. The secretary needs to provide only his or her present and former forenames and surnames and his or her residential address.

The *Register of Directors' Interests*, listing directors' holdings. This must include details of rights given to subscribe for shares or debentures, specifying the period during which they may be exercised and the consideration in cash or asset value. Further information must be entered when the rights are exercised.

The *Register of Charges* with details of mortgages and fixed and floating charges secured on the company's assets, consisting of a short description of the property charged, the amount of the charge and the names of the lenders, except in the case of securities to bearer.

The *Minute Book*. Proceedings at general meetings and directors' meetings must be recorded in minute books. When duly signed by the chairman, they are evidence of the proceedings.

The statutory books can be bound or looseleaf but precautions should be taken against falsification. They must be kept at the registered office or other place of business designated by the directors and available for inspection by shareholders without charge for at least two hours a day. Copies must be provided on payment of a fee. Creditors as well as shareholders are entitled to inspect copies of the instruments creating registrable charges and the register without charge and they can also be inspected by outsiders on payment of a fee. Access to minutes of directors' meetings is available only to the directors, the secretary and the auditors. The office may be closed and the books inaccessible for up to 30 days, provided you advertise the closure. A full list of the books, registers and documents which must be available for inspection is set out in Appendix 4.

For a full range of services for limited companies and their owners, contact your nearest DFK UK office:

1 Scotland
Sandy Mowat
0141 354 0354
smowat@dfkuk.com

2 North England
John Richards
0191 256 9500
jrichards@dfkuk.com

3 North West & East
James White
0113 246 1234
jwhite@dfkuk.com

4 Midlands
Steven Heathcote
0121 454 4141
sheathcote@dfkuk.com

5 South West and South Wales
Steve Fox
01225 428114
sfox@dfkuk.com

6 London & South East
Mark Lamb
020 7509 9000
mlamb@dfkuk.com

7 East Anglia
Peter Gardiner
01206 549303
pgardiner@dfkuk.com

8 South Coast
Neil Raynsford
023 8061 3000
nraynsford@dfkuk.com

9 Isle of Man
Gethin Taylor
01624 647171
gtaylor@dfkuk.com

10 Jersey
Peter Nicolle
01534 488 000
pnicolle@dfkuk.com

11 Ireland
James O'Connor
(353) (1) 6790 800
joconnor@dfkuk.com

Edinburgh

Glasgow

Newcastle

Isle of Man

Leeds

Dublin

Leicester

Birmingham

Northampton

Bristol

Colchester

Cork

Watford

Bath

London

Croydon

● Indicates DFK UK member firms office locations

Andover   Southampton   Reading   Hove

Jersey

National Coverage, Local Knowledge

DFK UK is a national network of independent accounting firms, established in 1996. It provides you with access to substantial resources in 22 commercial centres throughout the UK. With over 90 partners and more than 600 staff, we have experts who can advise on almost all financial matters.

The members of the group all meet and remain in communication with each other on a regular basis and work together to provide effective advice, assistance and solutions for your clients.

DFK UK's affiliation with DFK International enhances our worldwide reach, provides additional resources and expands the world of opportunity for your clients.

We look forward to discussing your business needs with you.

Mark Lamb
DFK UK Chairman

www.dfkuk.com

ANNUAL RETURN

Each year an annual return must be filed with the Registrar on Form 363a (see page 93). The return is made up to the 'return date', which is the anniversary of incorporation or, if the last return was made on a different date, on the anniversary of that date. The return basically summarises some of the information in the statutory books and changes during the year. This includes details of issued shares, a list of past and present shareholders, and details of directors and shadow directors (including their dates of birth) and of the secretary. Appointment of new directors, however, must be filed on Form 288a and the resignation or retirement of directors or the secretary and changes in their particulars on Forms 288b and 288c respectively (see pages 68–69). A change in the registered office address must be filed on Form 287.

The classification scheme giving a company's 'type' is the same as that used for VAT trade classification, with the addition of three extra codes. Copies of VAT trade classifications are available from your local VAT enquiry office free of charge.

A copy of the annual return signed by a director or the secretary must be sent to the Registrar, with the registration fee of £15, within 28 days of the return date.

If you have fewer than 21 shareholders, Companies House will send you its new 'shuttle' Annual Return Form 363s for following years. You must still list all the shareholders, but the company's capital and share-holder information is pre-printed and the form is sent with a covering letter stating when the return must be filed and what information, if any, is required to complete the return.

If an annual return is not filed, the company and the directors are liable to fines (see page 74).

THE ACCOUNTS

Accounting reference date

Your newly incorporated company's accounting reference date (ARD) – the date to which it will make up accounts each year – is the last day of the month in which the anniversary of incorporation falls plus or minus seven days. For instance, a company incorporated on 16 April

Companies House
— for the record —

Please complete in typescript,
or in bold black capitals.

CHFP000

363a

Annual Return

Company Number |

Company Name in full |

|

Date of this return
The information in this return is made up to

Day   Month   Year

|__|__|/|__|__|/|__|__|__|__|

Date of next return
If you wish to make your next return
to a date earlier than the anniversary
of this return please show the date here.
Companies House will then send a form
at the appropriate time.

Day   Month   Year

|__|__|/|__|__|/|__|__|__|__|

Registered Office
Show here the address **at the date of**
this return.

|

|

Any change of
registered office
must *be notified*
on form 287.

Post town |

County / Region |

UK Postcode |__|__|__|__| |__|__|__|

Principal business activities

Show trade classification code number(s)
for the principal activity or activities.

|_____ |_____

|_____ |_____

If the code number cannot be determined,
give a brief description of principal activity.

|

|

Companies House receipt date barcode

This form has been provided free of charge
by Companies House

Form April 2002

When you have completed and signed the form please send it to the
Registrar of Companies at:
Companies House, Crown Way, Cardiff, CF14 3UZ   DX 33050 Cardiff
for companies registered in England and Wales
or
Companies House, 37 Castle Terrace, Edinburgh, EH1 2EB
for companies registered in Scotland   **DX 235 Edinburgh**

Page 1

Figure 5.1   Annual return

Register of members

If the register of members is not kept at the registered office, state here where it is kept.

Post town

County / Region   UK Postcode ⌴⌴⌴⌴ ⌴⌴⌴

Register of Debenture holders

If there is a register of debenture holders, or a duplicate of any such register or part of it, which is not kept at the registered office, state here where it is kept.

Post town

County / Region   UK Postcode ⌴⌴⌴⌴ ⌴⌴⌴

Company type

Public limited company ☐

Private company limited by shares ☐

Private company limited by guarantee without share capital ☐

Private company limited by shares exempt under section 30 ☐

Private company limited by guarantee exempt under section 30 ☐

Private unlimited company with share capital ☐

Private unlimited company without share capital ☐

Please tick the appropriate box

Company Secretary

* Voluntary details.

(Please photocopy this area to provide details of joint secretaries).

†† Tick this box if the address shown is a service address for the beneficiary of a Confidentiality Order granted under section 723B of the Companies Act 1985 otherwise, give your usual residential address. In the case of a corporation or Scottish firm, give the registered or principal office address.

If a partnership give the names and addresses of the partners or the name of the partnership and office address.

Details of a new company secretary must be notified on form 288a.

Name   * Style / Title

Forename(s)

Surname

Address ††

Post town

County / Region   UK Postcode ⌴⌴⌴⌴ ⌴⌴⌴

Country

Page 2

Figure 5.1 *continued*

Directors

Details of new directors must be notified on form 288a

Please list directors in alphabetical order.

Name   * Style / Title

Directors In the case of a director that is a corporation or a Scottish firm, the name is the corporate or firm name.

Date of birth   Day   Month   Year

Forename(s)

†† Tick this box if the address shown is a service address for the beneficiary of a Confidentiality Order granted under section 723B of the Companies Act 1985 otherwise, give your usual residential address. In the case of a corporation or Scottish firm, give the registered or principal office address.

Surname

Address ††

Post town

County / Region   UK Postcode

Country   Nationality

Business occupation

* Voluntary details.

Name   * Style / Title

Directors In the case of a director that is a corporation or a Scottish firm, the name is the corporate or firm name.

Date of birth   Day   Month   Year

Forename(s)

†† Tick this box if the address shown is a service address for the beneficiary of a Confidentiality Order granted under section 723B of the Companies Act 1985 otherwise, give your usual residential address. In the case of a corporation or Scottish firm, give the registered or principal office address.

Surname

Address ††

Post town

County / Region   UK Postcode

Country   Nationality

Business occupation

Page 3

Figure 5.1 *continued*

Issued share capital	Class (e.g. Ordinary/Preference)	Number of shares issued	Aggregate Nominal Value (i.e Number of shares issued multiplied by nominal value per share, or total amount of stock)
Enter details of all the shares in issue at the date of this return.			
	_____	_____	_____
	_____	_____	_____
	_____	_____	_____
	_____	_____	_____
	Totals		
		_____	_____

List of past and present shareholders
(Use attached schedule where appropriate)
A full list is required if one was not included with either of the last two returns.

There were no changes in the period ☐

                on paper   in another format

A list of changes is enclosed ☐ ☐

A full list of shareholders is enclosed ☐ ☐

Certificate

I certify that the information given in this return is true to the best of my knowledge and belief.

Signed [_____] **Date** [_____]

† Please delete as appropriate.

† a director /secretary

When you have signed the return send it with the fee to the Registrar of Companies. Cheques should be made payable to **Companies House.**

This return includes [_____] continuation sheets.

(enter number)

You do not have to give any contact information in the box opposite but if you do, it will help Companies House to contact you if there is a query on the form. The contact information that you give will be visible to searchers of the public record.

_____

_____

_____ Tel _____

DX number |_____ DX exchange |_____

Figure 5.1 *continued*

Directors

Details of new directors must be notified on form 288a

Please list directors in alphabetical order.

Name   * Style / Title

Directors In the case of a director that is a corporation or a Scottish firm, the name is the corporate or firm name.

        Day   Month   Year

Date of birth   ∟∟/∟∟/∟∟∟∟

Forename(s)

†† Tick this box if the address shown is a service address for the beneficiary of a Confidentiality Order granted under section 723B of the Companies Act 1985 otherwise, give your usual residential address. In the case of a corporation or Scottish firm, give the registered or principal office address.

Surname

Address ††

Post town

County / Region   UK Postcode ∟∟∟∟   ∟∟∟

Country   **Nationality**

Business occupation

* Voluntary details.

Name   * Style / Title

Directors In the case of a director that is a corporation or a Scottish firm, the name is the corporate or firm name.

        Day   Month   Year

Date of birth   ∟∟/∟∟/∟∟∟∟

Forename(s)

†† Tick this box if the address shown is a service address for the beneficiary of a Confidentiality Order granted under section 723B of the Companies Act 1985 otherwise, give your usual residential address. In the case of a corporation or Scottish firm, give the registered or principal office address.

Surname

Address ††

Post town

County / Region   UK Postcode ∟∟∟∟   ∟∟∟

Country   **Nationality**

Business occupation

Page 5

Figure 5.1 *continued*

Directors

Please list directors in alphabetical order.

Details of new directors must be notified on form 288a

Directors In the case of a director that is a corporation or a Scottish firm, the name is the corporate or firm name.

†† Tick this box if the address shown is a service address for the beneficiary of a Confidentiality Order granted under section 723B of the Companies Act 1985 otherwise, give your usual residential address. In the case of a corporation or Scottish firm, give the registered or principal office address.

Name   * Style / Title

Day   Month   Year

Date of birth   └─└─/└─└─/└─└─└─└─

Forename(s)

Surname

Address ††

Post town

County / Region   UK Postcode   └─└─└─└─   └─└─└─

Country   **Nationality**

Business occupation

* Voluntary details.

Name   * Style / Title

Directors In the case of a director that is a corporation or a Scottish firm, the name is the corporate or firm name.

†† Tick this box if the address shown is a service address for the beneficiary of a Confidentiality Order granted under section 723B of the Companies Act 1985 otherwise, give your usual residential address. In the case of a corporation or Scottish firm, give the registered or principal office address.

Day   Month   Year

Date of birth   └─└─/└─└─/└─└─└─└─

Forename(s)

Surname

Address ††

Post town

County / Region   UK Postcode   └─└─└─└─   └─└─└─

Country   **Nationality**

Business occupation

Page 6

Figure 5.1 *continued*

2003 would have an ARD of 30 April and its accounts would cover the period from 30 April 2003 to 30 April 2004, plus or minus seven days. Accounts filed with a made-up date other than the ARD will be rejected by the Registrar and the company and directors will be liable to the fines set out in Appendix 4.

The first accounting reference period starts on incorporation and accounts covering 12 months or less must be delivered to the Registrar within 10 days of the ARD. Your first accounts can, however, cover a longer period and they must then be delivered to the Registrar within 22 months of the date of incorporation or three months from the ARD, whichever is the longer.

Deadlines are calculated to the exact day. If your company was incorporated on 1 December 2006 with an ARD of 31 December 2006, you have until midnight on 1 December 2007 to deliver the first account covering a period over 12 months. Subsequent periods begin after the end of the previous period and are for 12 months unless the date is changed on application to the Registrar on Form 225 (see page 101) during the accounting year or during the period allowed for delivery of the accounts to the Registrar or to the Secretary of State for Trade and Industry (see page 137).

Accounting records

The Companies Acts require companies to keep accounting records to show and explain company transactions and reflect the company's financial position with reasonable accuracy. The directors are responsible for ensuring that the balance sheet and profit and loss accounts are set out in the form prescribed in the Acts and that they give a 'true and fair view' of the company's financial position and its transactions.

Records must be maintained on a day-to-day basis to include:

- details of cash receipts and payments on a daily basis, including details of the transactions to which they relate;
- a list of assets and liabilities;
- a statement of stock of goods held at the end of (each) financial year with details of stock takings on which the records are based;
- with the exception of retailers, a sufficient description of goods and services bought and sold to enable sellers and purchasers to be identified.

Records must be retained for at least three years, but if you are registered for VAT they must be retained for a minimum of six years.

The company's accounts

Copies of the company's accounts, comprising the balance sheet, approved by the board and signed on their behalf by a director, the profit and loss account, the auditor's report and the director's report, approved by the board and signed on their behalf by a director or the secretary, must, unless the company has elected to dispense with this requirement (see page 112), be put before the shareholders in general meeting within 10 months of the end of the accounting reference period. Accounts must be dated and signed and identify the financial reporting framework, ie whether the auditors have used the EU International Accounting Standards (IAS) or UK GAPP. Any statement about accounting or filing exemptions must appear *above* the director's signature.

Twenty-one days before the meeting copies must be sent to all share and debenture holders and to anyone else entitled to be given notice of the meeting, such as the auditors, and copies must be sent to the Registrar. Share and debenture holders are also entitled to receive a free copy of the company's last accounts. There is, however, no requirement to lay the accounts before the shareholders or agree them with the Inland Revenue before they are filed.

The directors are liable to fines for delay in filing the accounts with the Registrar, depending on the length of the delay (see Appendix 4). Companies House sends a reminder before the deadline, which shows the filing deadline date in bold type. If the accounts are not filed on time a default notice and a demand for payment of the fine is delivered to the company's registered office within 14 days. Appeals against the fine are made first to the Registrar, then to the Complaints Adjudicator and thereafter to the county court.

The accounts must be in English but can be in Welsh if you trade in Wales, when an English translation must be annexed to the accounts sent to the Registrar.

The audit exemption

'Small' firms with a turnover not exceeding £5.6 million, assets of not more than £2.8 million and with an average of fewer than 51 employees

Companies House
— for the record —

225

Please complete in typescript,
or in bold black capitals

CHWP000

Change of accounting reference date

Company Number

Company Name in Full

	Day	Month	Year
The accounting reference period ending			

NOTES

You may use this form to change the accounting date relating to either the current or the immediately previous accounting period.

a. You **may not** change a period for which the accounts are already overdue.

b. You **may not** extend a period beyond 18 months unless the company is subject to an administration order.

c. You **may not** extend periods more than once in five years unless:

1. the company is subject to an administration order, or

2. you have the specific approval of the Secretary of State, (please enclose a copy), or

3. you are extending the company's accounting reference period to align with that of a parent or subsidiary undertaking established in the European Economic Area, or

4. the form is being submitted by an oversea company.

	Day	Month	Year
is **shortened** ☐ so as to end on **extended** ☐			

please tick appropriate box

Subsequent periods will end on the same day and month in future years.

If extending more than once in five years, please indicate in the box the number of the provision listed in note c. on which you are relying.

Signed _____ **Date** _____

† Please delete as appropriate

† a director / secretary / administrator / administrative receiver / receiver and manager / receiver (Scotland) / person authorised on behalf of an oversea company

You do not have to give any contact information in the box opposite but if you do, it will help Companies House to contact you if there is a query on the form. The contact information that you give will be visible to searchers of the public record.

	Tel
DX number	DX exchange

Companies House receipt date barcode

This form has been provided free of charge by Companies House.

10/03

When you have completed and signed the form please send it to the Registrar of Companies at:
Companies House, Crown Way, Cardiff, CF14 3UZ   **DX 33050 Cardiff**
for companies registered in England and Wales   **or**
Companies House, 37 Castle Terrace, Edinburgh, EH1 2EB   **DX 235 Edinburgh**
for companies registered in Scotland   **or LP - 4 Edinburgh 2**

Figure 5.2   Change of accounting reference date

Company Number

† Directors only.   †Other directorships

NOTES
Show the full forenames, NOT INITIALS. If the director or secretary is a corporation or Scottish firm, show the name on surname line and registered or principal office on the usual residential line.

Give previous forenames or surname(s) except:
- for a married woman, the name by which she was known before marriage need not be given.
- for names not used since the age of 18 or for at least 20 years

A peer or individual known by a title may state the title instead of or in addition to the forenames and surname and need not give the name by which that person was known before he or she adopted the title or succeeded to it.

Other directorships.
Give the name of every company incorporated in Great Britain of which the person concerned is a director or has been a director at any time in the past five years.

You may exclude a company which either is, or at all times during the past five years when the person concerned was a director, was
- dormant
- a parent company which wholly owned the company making the return, or
- another wholly owned subsidiary of the same parent company.

Figure 5.2 *continued*

can file unaudited accounts. Fulfilment of at least two of the criteria is sufficient to categorise the company. The requirement is only for an abbreviated balance sheet with explanatory notes. The full accounts can be filed, and the shareholders are entitled to see the profit and loss account and the directors' report. Some companies may have to prepare audited accounts to comply with the terms of their lease.

The balance sheet must include a statement by the directors referring to the relevant sections of the 1985 Act stating that:

- the company was entitled to the exemption;
- shareholders have not deposited a notice requiring an audit;
- the directors acknowledge their responsibility for:
  - ensuring the company keeps accounting records in compliance with the Companies Act 1985, and
  - preparing accounts giving a true and fair view of the company's affairs;
- advantage has been taken of the various exemptions – details must be listed for individual accounts;
- in the directors' opinion the company is entitled to take advantage of the exemption(s).

Shareholders with at least 10 per cent of the company's issued capital or at least 10 per cent of any class of shares are entitled to ask for an audit on giving written notice to the company's registered office at least one month before the end of the financial year.

If turnover exceeds £90,000 but is less than £1 million, the unaudited account must be accompanied by an accountant's report. This must state whether the accounts agree with the company's accounting records, whether they have been drawn up in compliance with the Companies Act 1985 as amended and whether the company is entitled to the exemption from audit.

NB Your Articles should be checked to ensure that you are not precluded from taking advantage of the audit exemptions.

The 'exemption for individual accounts': abbreviated accounts

'Small' companies, may file abbreviated accounts with the Registrar. The abbreviated accounts include a modified balance sheet, although full accounts must still be sent to share and debenture holders. The modified balance sheet must contain a statement by the directors, above their signatures, that they have relied on the exemption for individual accounts on the ground that the company is entitled to the benefit of them as a small company. A special auditors' report must also be filed, stating that in the auditors' opinion the requirements for exemption are satisfied. Their report must reproduce the full text of the auditors' report delivered to shareholders at the Annual General Meeting and annexed to the accounts circulated to shareholders.

The abbreviated accounts are an abbreviated version of the full balance sheet and aggregate amounts can be given for each item except for the figures relating to debtors and creditors. The debtors must be analysed to show separately for each item the amounts falling due after one year. The information required where the directors' total remuneration is at least £60,000 need not be set out, nor need there be a statement (as is required on the full accounts) that they have been prepared in accordance with applicable accounting standards. Accounting policies adopted by the company, details of share capital and debentures, particulars of allotments and the basis of conversion of foreign currency amounts into sterling must be included. Where appropriate, comparative details and figures must be given for the previous financial year.

Contents of the accounts

The accounts of the smaller company must include:

▪ The aggregate amount of directors' and shadow directors' emoluments (ie salaries, fees, commission payments, expenses, pension contributions and the estimated money value of benefits received in kind). If the total is £60,000 or more, the accounts must instead set out the chairperson's remuneration, amounts received by directors paid more than the chairperson and state the number of directors paid less than £5,000 and how many receive payments between successive multiples of £5,000. Details of total payments waived by directors and payments and benefits received from third parties must also be included.

▪ Details of loans, credit arrangements and agreements for loans and credit arrangements made by the company with the directors and shadow directors and of any company transactions in which they have a direct or indirect material interest. ('Material' interests are not material if a majority of the directors – other than the interested party – thinks they are not material.)

- Details of transactions with persons connected with directors and shadow directors. A 'connected' person is the partner, spouse, child or step-child of a director or shadow director. It is a company with which the director or shadow director is associated and of which he or she controls at least one-fifth of the voting shares, a trustee of a trust under which the director, shadow director or connected person is a beneficiary, and the partner of a connected person. Details of credit transactions, guarantees and securities given for credit arrangements which involve amounts up to £5,000 need not be included but credit facilities extended to company officers (excluding the directors) involving a total liability of £2,500 must be set out.
- Details of directors' share and debenture holdings, and of subscription rights granted to or exercised by the directors and their immediate family, although these can instead be included in the directors' report.

The *directors' report*, approved by the board and signed by a director or the secretary, need not be filed with the small company's accounts but the directors must report to shareholders. Their report must give a fair review of the development of business during the financial year and of the position at the year end. It must also state the amount recommended as dividend and the amount, if any, that the directors propose to carry to reserve or retain for investment.

In addition, the report must name the directors and state the company's principal activities and any change in the activities during the year. Significant changes in the fixed assets must be listed, as well as details of directors' interests in shares or debentures at the beginning and end of the year. Details must also be given of any important events affecting the company business and of research and development. Certain details of share transactions, employee training and welfare, and political and charitable contributions must also be specified.

The auditors are required to review the report, so you should ask them for assistance in ensuring that everything that materially affects the company's affairs is included.

Unless you claim audit exemption you must also file a special auditors' report and the auditors', special auditors' or accountants' report must state the names of the auditors or accountants who sign and date their report.

DISCLOSING THE ACCOUNTS

The company's accounting records must be kept at the registered office or another office designated by the directors and be open to inspection by the company's officers at all times.

It is an offence to mislead the auditors and they are entitled to access to all the necessary documents and information in the preparation of the accounts.

AUDITORS

The auditors can be appointed before the first general meeting at which the accounts are to be presented. They stay in office until the end of that meeting unless removed by ordinary (majority) vote of the shareholders. They must be appointed or re-appointed at every Annual General Meeting for a term running from the conclusion of the meeting before which the accounts are laid until the end of the next AGM.

If for any reason the company is without an auditor, the directors or the company in general meeting can appoint a temporary replacement. If one is not appointed by the meeting the company must notify the Secretary of State within seven days of the meeting, when the Secretary of State may make the appointment.

The auditors must be members of the Institute of Chartered Accountants in England and Wales, Scotland or Ireland or of the Chartered Association of Certified Accountants. A director or employee cannot be the company's auditor but the auditor can act as the company's accountant, preparing company accounts and VAT and PAYE returns and generally giving secretarial assistance and taxation advice.

Responsibility for the proper administration of company affairs, however, rests with the directors. The auditors' only responsibility is for any loss caused by their own negligence or fraud. Their reports and conclusions must be based on proper investigation and they are entitled to access to all necessary documents and information. If they are not satisfied that your books and accounts properly reflect the company's financial circumstances, this must be stated in their report.

THE COMPANY SEAL

The company seal – usually a metal disc with the full name of the company on it in raised letters – used to be required as the company's 'signature' and was impressed on documents that have to be made by deed. These include commercial contracts, leases, share certificates, debentures and mortgages. Two directors or a director and the company secretary also had to sign the document for and on behalf of the company.

Now, the signatures of the two directors or the director and company secretary, signing for and on behalf of the company, has the same effect as if the document had been executed (signed) under seal.

If you want to use a seal, its use must be authorised by the directors and you will have to adopt an appropriate Article to provide that affixing the seal must be evidenced by the signature of a director and the company secretary.

SHARE ISSUES

The directors must ensure that the Articles are complied with on share issues. The secretary records the issue of shares in the minutes of the meeting at which they are issued, and makes the appropriate entries in the Register of members to show the new shareholders' names and addresses and details of the shares issued.

Entries in the minutes and Register must also be made when shares are transferred.

SHARE CERTIFICATES

The secretary completes share certificates, which are numbered and state the number and class of shares issued. The certificate is signed by a director and the secretary and, if required by the Articles, sealed with the company seal.

MEETINGS

The method of calling and running meetings is set out in the Articles but procedure is more closely regulated for full company/shareholders' meetings than for directors' meetings, which can be run in any way that the directors think fit.

When the Company Law Reform Act comes into force private companies will not have to hold Annual General Meetings. Contact with shareholders can be via e-mail and shareholders' decisions can be made on written resolutions by simple or 75 per cent majority.

Single-member companies

The single-member company must, like any other company, have at least one director and a secretary who cannot also be the sole director. However, notwithstanding anything in the Articles to the contrary, the single member, present in person or by proxy, constitutes a quorum for meetings. A single-member 'shareholders' meeting' must be minuted as such and decisions must be formally notified to the company in writing, unless made by way of a written resolution.

If a contract between the company and a single shareholder who is also a director is not in writing, the terms of the contract must, unless the contract is made in the ordinary course of the company's business, be set out in a memorandum or recorded in the minutes of the next directors' meeting.

The 1989 Companies Act has simplified procedures for private companies and the relevant provisions are set out on page 112. They substantially reduce administration and costs and are particularly useful if there is a major overlap between ownership and management.

The following paragraphs apply, however, if you do not choose to take advantage of the new provisions.

THE FIRST BOARD MEETING

No notice is prescribed for calling board meetings. Provided all the directors are notified they can decide to dispense with meetings, conducting business by telephone or correspondence. Table A includes a provision enabling written resolutions signed by all the directors to be as valid and effective as those passed at a duly convened and held meeting of directors. Otherwise, oral notice is sufficient and if a meeting is called a majority of the directors must attend; if a quorum is required by the Articles, the specified number of directors must be present.

The company exists from the date the Registrar issues the Certificate of Incorporation. However, a great deal of important company business cannot be dealt with until the first board meeting and it should therefore be held on the same day as, or as soon as possible after, incorporation.

Business will include:

- A report on the incorporation of the company. The Certificate of Incorporation should be produced.
- Reporting the appointment of the first directors and secretary.
- Appointing the chairperson.
- Appointing any additional directors.
- Reporting on the situation of the registered office and deciding whether it should be changed.
- Adopting the company seal and confirming the authorised users and signatories.
- Agreeing the opening of the bank account and naming the signatories, for instance any two directors or a director and the secretary. Your bank will provide a form of company mandate (agreement) which sets out the necessary wording. This must be sent to them with a copy of the Memorandum and Articles of Association and they will want to see the Certificate of Incorporation.
- The allotment of shares (other than the subscribers' shares) and a record of receipts of any payment received for the subscribers' shares and for any other shares allotted. Sealing of share certificates must be minuted.
- Appointing the auditors and deciding on the accounting reference date.

You may also want to appoint a managing director or chairperson, appoint solicitors, deal with matters relating to the company's trading activities and with general administrative matters, and disclose the directors' interests in contracts.

The meeting must be minuted by the secretary but minutes of directors'/board meetings are not available for shareholders' inspection. They should therefore be kept in a Minute Book separate from that used for minutes of company (shareholders') meetings.

GENERAL MEETINGS

The shareholders acting together in general meeting can do anything *intra vires* (within the powers of) the company as set out in its Memorandum and Articles of Association. In practice, their power to control the company is delegated to the directors and exercised by resolutions passed in general meeting.

The secretary must keep minutes of meetings in the Minute Book kept for that purpose and when signed by the chairperson of the meeting or the next successive meeting, they are evidence of the proceedings.

VOTING

The Articles usually provide that voting is by a show of hands; each member, regardless of his shareholding, then has one vote. The Articles also usually provide that the chairperson, or any two members, or a member or members holding not less than one-tenth of the total voting rights, can demand a poll when voting is normally on the basis of one vote per share held. Special voting rights attached to shares are taken into account before deciding whether a motion has been carried on a poll, and usually a proxy (authorised by an absent shareholder to vote on his behalf) can only vote on a poll.

A director's personal interest in a company contract disqualifies him from voting; if he does, the transaction can be set aside.

THE ANNUAL GENERAL MEETING

This must be held within 18 months of incorporation and once in every subsequent calendar year, 15 months being the longest permitted interval between meetings.

The meeting is more formal than a board meeting and motions must be proposed, seconded and voted on. The main business comprises:

- receiving the accounts and the directors' report;
- proposing the dividend;
- electing directors and re-electing those who retire by rotation;
- appointing or re-electing auditors and fixing their remuneration.

The holders of at least one-twentieth of the voting shares can force the company to present a resolution at the Annual General Meeting and to send their comments about it to all the shareholders. In exceptional circumstances a single director or shareholder can ask the court to order a meeting.

EXTRAORDINARY GENERAL MEETINGS

Any other company business is usually 'special' and requires an Extraordinary General Meeting, with notice to shareholders of what is to be discussed. The meeting is usually convened by the secretary, on the directors' instructions, to deal with business that cannot await the next Annual General Meeting.

Subject to the Articles, two or more holders of more than one-tenth of the fully paid-up voting shares can demand that the directors call a meeting within 21 days. In default, a meeting can be called by at least half of those shareholders within three months of the request.

NOTICE OF MEETINGS

Notice of meetings and of what is to be discussed must be given to shareholders and to the auditors in accordance with the provisions of the Articles. They usually specify 21 days for the Annual General Meeting and for meetings called to consider a special resolution, and 14 days for other meetings.

You must give 28 days' notice of a resolution to appoint new auditors or prevent their re-appointment and to remove or replace directors. Notice of the resolution must be given at least 21 days before the meeting, so it is usually convenient to give notice of the meeting and of the resolution at the same time.

Notice is given when posted and assumed to be delivered, but it is safest to include a provision in the Articles that an accidental omission to give notice, or its non-receipt, will not invalidate proceedings at meetings. Usually, you do not have to give notice to shareholders living abroad.

Notice can be waived with the consent of 95 per cent of the holders of voting shares and they can agree not to meet at all, but all shareholders with voting rights must agree before you can dispense with notice of the Annual General Meeting.

RESOLUTIONS

Resolutions may be ordinary, special or extraordinary.

Ordinary resolutions are passed by a straight majority of those actually present at the meeting. *Special and extraordinary resolutions* need a three-quarters majority and special resolutions must include proxy votes.

Most company business, including the removal of directors and a voluntary winding up in the circumstances specified in the Articles, requires only an ordinary resolution. Special resolutions are necessary to change the Articles and the company's name or objects and reduce its capital. Extraordinary resolutions are only needed for a voluntary winding up when the company is insolvent and for reconstructions and mergers.

Copies of special and extraordinary resolutions must be sent to the Registrar within 15 days of the meeting; draft forms of resolutions are set out in Appendix 5.

DEREGULATION OF PRIVATE COMPANIES – THE SIMPLIFIED PROCEDURES

You do not have to serve notice of resolutions and call and hold meetings, provided the action to be taken can be approved by the company, or any class of its shareholders, in general meeting and provided the resolution is signed by all shareholders entitled to vote at the meeting.

The provisions cover special, extraordinary and elective (see below) resolutions which take effect notwithstanding any provision in the Articles. The proposed written resolution must be sent to the auditors. It is only valid if they endorse their statement to the effect that it does not affect them as auditors, or that it does affect them but in their opinion need not be discussed in a general or class meeting, or they make no statement within seven days of receiving it.

The resolution must be minuted as if passed in a meeting and, when signed by a director or the secretary, is evidence that it has been passed in accordance with the Act. It must be filed with the Registrar if this is required for such a resolution passed in a general or class meeting.

However, there are some exceptions to, and adaptations of, the procedure. For instance, written resolutions cannot be used to remove directors or auditors before the end of their term of office, and there are special procedural requirements for:

- written resolutions for the disapplication of pre-emption rights;
- the provision of financial assistance to enable the company to buy its own shares;
- approval of payments out of capital;
- directors' service contracts and their business expenses.

ELECTIVE RESOLUTIONS

With the shareholders' unanimous agreement at a properly convened general meeting, or their unanimous written consent, the company can elect to:

- have no Annual General Meeting;
- dispense with the requirement to lay accounts before shareholders;
- vote annually to appoint auditors;
- give directors an indefinite authority (ie beyond the five-year limit) to allot shares;
- reduce the majority required for consent to short notice of meeting to 90 per cent.

6

Changes after incorporation

Changes made after incorporation involve formalities, and some decisions can only be made by the shareholders in general meeting and necessitate filing forms and copy documents with the Registrar.

The directors are responsible for keeping the Registrar informed and there are penalties if some of the documentation is not filed.

Some of the documentation must be signed by a director and/or the company secretary and some by the chairperson of the relevant meeting. The documents you are most likely to use are discussed in this chapter and listed in Appendix 3 and draft forms of resolutions are set out in Appendix 5.

You can now file notices, copies of accounts and reports with Companies House electronically, that is, via telephone, fax, e-mail or by posting them on a website.

You can also send the accounts, summary financial statements and reports electronically to shareholders, debenture-holders and auditors or, provided you notify the recipients, publish them on your website for at least 21 days before the general meeting at which they are to be laid. Notification that notices are on a website must contain specified details about the meeting and the shareholders can send proxy forms and other notices to you via e-mail.

CHANGE OF DIRECTORS AND SECRETARY

Directors are elected, re-elected and removed by a majority vote on an ordinary resolution put before the shareholders in general meeting but the shareholders do not vote on the appointment or removal of the company secretary.

Two directors can be appointed in one resolution, and notice of a resolution to prevent re-appointment or to remove or replace serving directors must be sent to shareholders at least 28 days before the meeting. Notice must also be given to the person concerned and to the auditors.

A director can put his or her objections to removal to the shareholders' meeting or require the company to circulate his or her written representations. The notice of the resolution sent to shareholders should then state that he or she has made written representations.

Changes of directors and secretary must be filed with the Registrar on Form 288b (see page 68), which incorporates a form of consent to act which must be signed by the new officer. Changes in their particulars must be filed on Form 288c (see page 69). It is the directors' responsibility to ensure that the Registrar is notified of a change of directors or company secretary.

CHANGING THE AUDITORS

An auditor is appointed at each Annual General Meeting to hold office from the conclusion of the meeting until the conclusion of the next AGM. He or she must be a member of the Institute of Chartered Accountants in England and Wales, Scotland or Ireland, or a member of the Association of Certified and Corporate Accountants (see page 106). Remuneration, including expenses, is fixed by the shareholders in general meeting.

Appointment is by ordinary resolution of the shareholders and can be made at any time before the expiry of the term of office agreed separately with the directors. The auditor may be entitled to compensation for premature termination of the separate agreement.

A retiring auditor or one removed before the expiration of his or her term of office may address the meeting called to appoint a successor, or require the company to circulate comments to shareholders. The resolution for the replacement should state that the retiring auditor has made written representations. He or she is also entitled to attend company meetings which discuss matters dealt with during his or her term of office.

The directors or the company in general meeting can fill casual vacancies but the appointment must be confirmed by resolution at the Annual General Meeting. Unless the court orders otherwise, a copy of the auditor's statement must be sent to the Registrar.

Special notice of 28 days is required for resolutions appointing new auditors, and to reappoint an auditor appointed to fill a casual vacancy or to remove one before expiry of his or her term of office.

Notice of removal of the auditors must be sent to the Registrar on Form 391 within 14 days of the meeting.

The auditor is entitled to attend all meetings of the company and to receive all notes of, and other communications relating to, meetings which are sent to shareholders.

CHANGE OF REGISTERED OFFICE

Changes must be notified to the Registrar, within 14 days of the change, on Form 287 (see page 122).

CHANGE IN THE PLACE WHERE STATUTORY BOOKS AND OTHER 'PUBLIC' DOCUMENTS ARE KEPT

Notices of any change in the place where the Register of Members (Form 353 – see page 123), copies of directors' service contracts (Form 318 – see page 124) and their interests in shares (Form 325 – see page 125) are kept must be filed with the Registrar within 14 days of the change. No time limit is specified for filing a notice of a change in the place where the Register of Debenture Holders (Form 190 – see page 128) is kept.

CHANGE OF NAME

The company's name is changed by majority vote of the shareholders on a special resolution. A copy of the signed resolution must be sent to

Companies House
— *for the record* —

10

Please complete in typescript,
or in bold black capitals.

CHWP000

Notes on completion appear on final page

First directors and secretary and intended situation of registered office

Company Name in full

Proposed Registered Office

(PO Box numbers only, are not acceptable)

Post town

County / Region   Postcode

If the memorandum is delivered by an agent for the subscriber(s) of the memorandum mark the box opposite and give the agent's name and address.

Agent's Name

Address

Post town

County / Region   Postcode

Number of continuation sheets attached

You do not have to give any contact information in the box opposite but if you do, it will help Companies House to contact you if there is a query on the form. The contact information that you give will be visible to searchers of the public record.

Tel

DX number   DX exchange

Companies House receipt date barcode

This form is been provided free of charge by Companies House

v 08/02

When you have completed and signed the form please send it to the Registrar of Companies at:

Companies House, Crown Way, Cardiff, CF14 3UZ   DX 33050 Cardiff
for companies registered in England and Wales
or
Companies House, 37 Castle Terrace, Edinburgh, EH1 2EB
for companies registered in Scotland   **DX 235 Edinburgh**

Figure 6.1   Notice of passing of resolution removing an auditor

Company Secretary (see notes 1-5)

Company name		

NAME   *Style / Title   *Honours etc

* Voluntary details

Forename(s)

Surname

Previous forename(s)

Previous surname(s)

Address

Usual residential address
For a corporation, give the
registered or principal office
address.   Post town

County / Region   Postcode

Country

I consent to act as secretary of the company named on page 1

Consent signature   **Date**

Directors (see notes 1-5)

Please list directors in alphabetical order

NAME   *Style / Title   *Honours etc

Forename(s)

Surname

Previous forename(s)

Previous surname(s)

Address

Usual residential address
For a corporation, give the
registered or principal office
address.   Post town

County / Region   Postcode

Country

Day   Month   Year

Date of birth   **Nationality**

Business occupation

Other directorships

I consent to act as director of the company named on page 1

Consent signature   **Date**

Figure 6.1 *continued*

Directors (continued) (see notes 1-5)

NAME	*Style / Title	*Honours etc
* Voluntary details	Forename(s)	
	Surname	
	Previous forename(s)	
	Previous surname(s)	
Address		

Usual residential address
For a corporation, give the
registered or principal office
address.

Post town	
County / Region	Postcode
Country	

	Day	Month	Year		
Date of birth				Nationality	

Business occupation

Other directorships

I consent to act as director of the company named on page 1

| Consent signature | | Date | |

This section must be signed by
Either

an agent on behalf
of all subscribers

Signed   Date

Or the subscribers

Signed   Date

(*i.e those who signed*
as members on the
memorandum of
association).

Signed   Date

Signed   Date

Signed   Date

Signed   Date

Signed   Date

Figure 6.1 *continued*

the Registrar within 15 days of the meeting with the £10 fee for entry on the Index or £80 for a same-day change. The restrictions on your choice are set out in Appendix 1. The change is effective from the date of the issue by the Registrar of an altered Certificate of Incorporation.

INCREASES IN CAPITAL AND ALLOTMENT OF SHARES

The company's authorised capital can be increased by ordinary resolution authorising the increase. A copy of the signed resolution and Form 123 (see page 131) must be sent to the Registrar within 15 days of the resolution and no capital duty is payable.

Within a month of the allotment of shares a Return of Allotments form, signed by a director or the secretary, must be filed with the Registrar. If the shares are issued for cash, the form to be completed is 88(2) – see page 133; otherwise Form 88(3) – see page 34 – must be filed together with a copy of the contract of sale or details specified on the form.

If the new issue varies the rights of existing shareholders it should be done through a *scheme of arrangement*, whether their rights are contained in the Memorandum or the Articles. The procedure involves an application to the court so you should take expert advice before taking action; dissenting shareholders can put their objections to the variation both to the court and at the shareholders' meeting.

THE DIRECTORS' AUTHORITY TO ALLOT SHARES

The directors' authority to allot shares expires five years from the date of incorporation or not more than five years after the date of adoption of an Article giving them the authority. Giving them authority, or varying, revoking or renewing it, requires the written consent of three-quarters of the shareholders or their consent given on an extraordinary resolution in general meeting.

The resolution must state or restate the amount of shares which may be allotted under the authority, or the amount remaining to be allotted under it, and must specify the date on which an authority or amended

---

Companies House
— for the record —

Please complete in typescript,
or in bold black capitals.
CHWP000

287

Change in situation or address of Registered Office

Company Number [   ]

Company Name in full [   ]
[   ]

New situation of registered office

NOTE:

The change in the situation of the registered office does not take effect until the Registrar has registered this notice.

For 14 days beginning with the date that a change of registered office is registered, a person may validly serve any document on the company at its previous registered office.

PO Box numbers only are not acceptable.

Address [   ]
[   ]

Post town [   ]

County / Region [   ] **Postcode** [   ]

Signed [   ] **Date** [   ]

† Please delete as appropriate.

You do not have to give any contact information in the box opposite but if you do, it will help Companies House to contact you if there is a query on the form. The contact information that you give will be visible to searchers of the public record.

† a director / secretary / administrator / administrative receiver / liquidator / receiver manager / receiver

[   ]

Tel

DX number   DX exchange

Companies House receipt date barcode

This form has been provided free of charge by Companies House.

10/03

When you have completed and signed the form please send it to the Registrar of Companies at:
Companies House, Crown Way, Cardiff, CF14 3UZ
for companies registered in England and Wales   or   **DX 33050 Cardi**
Companies House, 37 Castle Terrace, Edinburgh, EH1 2EB   **DX 235 Edinburgh**
for companies registered in Scotland   **or LP - 4 Edinburgl**

Figure 6.2 Change in situation or address of Registered Office

Companies House
— for the record —

353

Please complete in typescript,
or in bold black capitals.

CHWP000

Register of members

Company Number

Company Name in full

The register of members is kept at:

NOTE:
The register **MUST** be kept at an address in the country of incorporation.

This notice is not required where the register has, at all times since it came into existence (or in the case of a register in existence on 1 July 1948 at all times since then) been kept at the registered office.

Address

Post town

County / Region   **Postcode**

Signed   **Date**

† Please delete as appropriate.

† a director / secretary / administrator / administrative receiver / receiver manager / receiver

You do not have to give any contact information in the box opposite but if you do, it will help Companies House to contact you if there is a query on the form. The contact information that you give will be visible to searchers of the public record.

Tel

DX number   DX exchange

Companies House receipt date barcode

This form has been provided free of charge by Companies House.

Form revised 10/03

When you have completed and signed the form please send it to the Registrar of Companies at:
Companies House, Crown Way, Cardiff, CF14 3UZ   DX 33050 Cardiff
for companies registered in England and Wales
or
Companies House, 37 Castle Terrace, Edinburgh, EH1 2EB
for companies registered in Scotland   DX 235 Edinburgh
                                               or LP - 4 Edinburgh 2

Figure 6.3   Register of members

Companies House
— for the record —

318

Location of directors' service contracts

Please complete in typescript,
or in bold black capitals.

CHFP000

Company Number

Company Name in full

Address where directors' service contracts
or memoranda are available for inspection
by members.

NOTE:
Directors' service
contracts **MUST** be kept
at an address in the
country of incorporation.

This notice is not
required where the
relevant documents are
and have always been
kept at the Registered
Office.

Address

Post town

County / Region   Postcode

Signed   **Date**

† Please delete as appropriate.

Please give the name, address,
telephone number and, if available,
a DX number and Exchange of
the person Companies House should
contact if there is any query.

† a director / secretary / administrator / administrative receiver / receiver manager / receiver

Tel

DX number   DX exchange

Companies House receipt date barcode

This form has been provided free of charge
by Companies House.

Form revised July 1998

When you have completed and signed the form please send it to the
Registrar of Companies at:
Companies House, Crown Way, Cardiff, CF14 3UZ   **DX 33050 Cardiff**
for companies registered in England and Wales
or
Companies House, 37 Castle Terrace, Edinburgh, EH1 2EB
for companies registered in Scotland   **DX 235 Edinburgh**

Figure 6.4   Location of directors' service contracts

Companies House
— *for the record* —

325

Location of register of directors' interests in shares etc.

Please complete in typescript,
or in bold black capitals.

CHFP000

Company Number

Company Name in full

The register of directors' interests in shares and/or debentures is kept at:

NOTE:
The register **MUST** be kept at an address in the country of incorporation.

This notice is not required where the register is and has always been kept at the Registered Office.

Address

Post town

County / Region

Postcode

Signed

Date

† Please delete as appropriate.

† a director / secretary / administrator / administrative receiver / receiver manager / receiver

Please give the name, address, telephone number and, if available, a DX number and Exchange of the person Companies House should contact if there is any query.

Tel

DX number   DX exchange

Companies House receipt date barcode

This form has been provided free of charge by Companies House.

Form revised July 1998

When you have completed and signed the form please send it to the Registrar of Companies at:
Companies House, Crown Way, Cardiff, CF14 3UZ   **DX 33050 Cardiff**
for companies registered in England and Wales
or
Companies House, 37 Castle Terrace, Edinburgh, EH1 2EB
for companies registered in Scotland   **DX 235 Edinburgh**

Figure 6.5   Location of register of directors' interests in shares, etc

COMPANIES FORM No. 325a

G

CHFP000

Notice of place for inspection of a register of directors' interests in shares etc. which is kept in a non-legible form, or of any change in that place

325a

Please do not write in this margin

Pursuant to the Companies (Registers and Other Records) Regulations 1985

Note: For use only when the register is kept by computer or in some other non-legible form

Please complete legibly, preferably in black type, or bold block lettering

To the Registrar of Companies
(Address overleaf)

For official use

Company number

* insert full name of company

Name of company

*

gives notice, in accordance with regulation 3(1) of the Companies (Registers and Other Records)

Regulations 1985, that the place for inspection of the register of directors' interests in shares and/or

† delete as appropriate

debentures which the company keeps in a non-legible form is [now] †:

Postcode

† delete as appropriat

Signed   [Director][Secretary]†   Date

Presenter's name address and reference (if any) :

For official Use (02/06)
General Section

Post room

Figure 6.6   Notice of place for inspection of a register of holders of debentures which is kept in a non-legible form, or of any change in that place

Notes

The address for companies registered in England and Wales or Wales is :-

The Registrar of Companies
Companies House
Crown Way
Cardiff
CF14 3UZ

or, for companies registered in Scotland :-

The Registrar of Companies
Companies House
37 Castle Terrace
Edinburgh
EH1 2EB

Figure 6.6 *continued*

Companies House
— *for the record* —

190

Location of register of debenture holders

Please complete in typescript,
or in bold black capitals.
CHWP000

Company Number

Company Name in full

gives notice that †[a register][registers]†[in duplicate form] of holders of
debentures of the company of the classes mentioned below †[is][are]kept at:

NOTE:
This notice is not
required where the
register is, and has
always been, kept at
the Registered Office

Address

Post town

County / region

Postcode

Brief description of class of debentures

Signed

Date

† Please delete as appropriate.

† a director / secretary

You do not have to give any contact
information in the box opposite but
if you do, it will help Companies
House to contact you if there is a
query on the form. The contact
information that you give will be
visible to searchers of the public
record.

Tel

DX number   DX exchange

Companies House receipt date barcode

**This form has been provided free of charge
by Companies House.**

Form revised 10/03

When you have completed and signed the form please send it to the
Registrar of Companies at:
Companies House, Crown Way, Cardiff, CF14 3UZ   DX 33050 Cardiff
for companies registered in England and Wales
or
Companies House, 37 Castle Terrace, Edinburgh, EH1 2EB
for companies registered in Scotland   DX 235 Edinburgh
                                                          or LP - 4 Edinburgh 2

Figure 6.7   Location of register of debenture holders

G

CHWP000

COMPANIES FORM No. 190a

**Notice of place for inspection of
a register of holders of debentures
which is kept in a non-legible form,
or of any change in that place**

190a

Please do not
write in
this margin

Pursuant to the Companies (Registers and Other Records) Regulations 1985

Note: For use only when the register is kept by computer or in some other non-legible form

*Please complete
legibly, preferably
in black type, or
bold block lettering*

To the Registrar of Companies
(Address overleaf)

Name of company

For official use   Company number

* insert full name
of company

*

gives notice, in accordance with regulation 5(1) of the Companies (Registers and Other Records)

Regulations 1985, that the place for inspection of the register of debenture holders which the company

keeps in a non-legible form is [now]:

Postcode

Signed   [Director][Secretary]†   Date

† delete as
appropriate

Presenter's name address and
reference (if any) :

For official Use (02/06)
General Section   Post room

Figure 6.8   Notice of place for inspection of a register of holders of debentures which is kept in a non-legible form, or of any change in that place

Notes

The address for companies registered in England and Wales or Wales is :-

The Registrar of Companies
Companies House
Crown Way
Cardiff
CF14 3UZ
DX 33050 Cardiff

or, for companies registered in Scotland :-

The Registrar of Companies
Companies House
37 Castle Terrace
Edinburgh
EH1 2EB

DX 235 Edinburgh
or LP - 4 Edinburgh 2

Figure 6.8 *continued*

G

COMPANIES FORM No. 123

**Notice of increase
in nominal capital**

123

CHWP000

Please do not
write in
this margin

Pursuant to section 123 of the Companies Act 1985

*Please complete
legibly, preferably
in black type, or
bold block lettering*

To the Registrar of Companies
(Address overleaf)

For official use   Company number

Name of company

* insert full name
  of company

*

gives notice in accordance with section 123 of the above Act that by resolution of the company

dated _____ the nominal capital of the company has been

increased by £ _____ beyond the registered capital of £ _____.

† the copy must be
printed or in some
other form approved
by the registrar

A copy of the resolution authorising the increase is attached. †

The conditions (eg. voting rights, dividend rights, winding-up rights etc.) subject to which the new

shares have been or are to be issued are as follows :

Please tick here if
continued overleaf

‡ Insert
Director,
Secretary,
Administrator,
Administrative
Receiver or
Receiver
(Scotland) as
appropriate

Signed   Designation ‡   Date

Presenter's name address and
reference (if any) :

For official Use (02/06)
General Section

Post room

Figure 6.9 Notice of increase in nominal capital

Notes

The address for companies registered in England and Wales or Wales is :-

The Registrar of Companies
Companies House
Crown Way
Cardiff
CF14 3UZ

DX 33050 Cardiff

or, for companies registered in Scotland :-

The Registrar of Companies
Companies House
37 Castle Terrace
Edinburgh
EH1 2EB

DX 235 Edinburgh or LP - 4 Edinburgh 2

Figure 6.9 *continued*

Companies House
— for the record —

Please complete in typescript, or in bold black capitals.

CHWP000

Company Number

Company name in full

88(2)

(Revised 2005)

Return of Allotment of Shares

Shares allotted (including bonus shares):
(see Guidance Booklet GBA6)

	From			To		
Date or period during which shares were allotted (If shares were allotted on one date enter that date in the "from" box)	Day	Month	Year	Day	Month	Year

Class of shares
(ordinary or preference etc)

Number allotted

Nominal value of each share

Amount (if any) paid or due on each share (including any share premium)

List the names and addresses of the allottees and the number and class of shares allotted to each overleaf

If the allotted shares (including bonus shares) are fully or partly paid up otherwise than in cash please state:

% that each share is to be treated as paid up

% (if any) that each share is to be paid up in cash

Consideration for which the shares were allotted
(This information must be supported by the original or a certified copy of the contract or by Form 88(3) if the contract is not in writing)

Companies House receipt date barcode

This form has been provided free of charge by Companies House.

09/2005

When you have completed and signed the form please send it to the Registrar of Companies at:

Companies House, Crown Way, Cardiff, CF14 3UZ   DX 33050 Cardiff
for companies registered in England and Wales   or
Companies House, 37 Castle Terrace, Edinburgh, EH1 2EB   DX 235 Edinburgh
for companies registered in Scotland   or LP - 4 Edinburgh 2

Figure 6.10   Return of allotment of shares

Names and addresses of the allottees

Shareholder details *(list joint allottees as one shareholder)*	Shares and share class allotted	
Name(s) _____ Address _____ _____ UK Postcode ⌐ ⌐ ⌐ ⌐ ⌐ ⌐ ⌐	Class of shares allotted _____ _____ _____	Number allotted _____ _____ _____
Name(s) _____ Address _____ _____ UK Postcode ⌐ ⌐ ⌐ ⌐ ⌐ ⌐ ⌐	Class of shares allotted _____ _____ _____	Number allotted _____ _____ _____
Name(s) _____ Address _____ _____ UK Postcode ⌐ ⌐ ⌐ ⌐ ⌐ ⌐ ⌐	Class of shares allotted _____ _____ _____	Number allotted _____ _____ _____
Name(s) _____ Address _____ _____ UK Postcode ⌐ ⌐ ⌐ ⌐ ⌐ ⌐ ⌐	Class of shares allotted _____ _____ _____	Number allotted _____ _____ _____
Name(s) _____ Address _____ _____ UK Postcode ⌐ ⌐ ⌐ ⌐ ⌐ ⌐ ⌐	Class of shares allotted _____ _____ _____	Number allotted _____ _____ _____

Please enter the number of continuation sheets (if any) attached to this form   ☐

Signed _____   Date _____

** A director / secretary / administrator / administrative receiver / receiver /
official receiver / receiver manager / voluntary arrangement supervisor   ** *Please delete as appropriate*

Contact Details

You do not have to give any contact information in the box opposite but if you do, it will help Companies House to contact you if there is a query on the form. The contact information that you give will be visible to searchers of the public record.

Tel
DX number   DX exchange

Figure 6.10   *continued*

Figure 6.11 Cancellation of alteration to the objects of a company

authority will expire. A copy of the signed resolution must be sent to the Registrar within 15 days of the passing of the resolution.

CHANGES IN THE MEMORANDUM OF ASSOCIATION

Alteration of the *objects clause* requires the approval of 75 per cent of the shareholders to a special resolution.

Application to cancel the alteration can be made to the court within 21 days of the resolution by the holders of 15 per cent of the shares. If there is no objection the alteration is valid. A printed copy of the amended Memorandum, together with a copy of the signed resolution authorising the change, must be sent to the Registrar, but the change is not effective until the Registrar has advertised it in the *Gazette*.

CHANGES IN THE ARTICLES OF ASSOCIATION

Alterations in the Articles are by a majority vote of the shareholders on a special resolution. However, if the company has two or more classes of shares, and the alteration affects the rights attached to any class, it should be done through a scheme of arrangement.

Printed and signed copies of resolutions altering the Articles must be sent to the Registrar within 15 days of the resolution but the alteration is not effective until the Registrar has advertised it in the *Gazette*.

CHANGING THE ACCOUNTING REFERENCE DATE

You can change the ARD by shortening or extending (to a maximum of 18 months) the accounting period (which fixes your accounting year). You can shorten the period as often and by as many months as you like. You cannot extend the period to more than 18 months from the start date and cannot extend it more than once in five years unless:

- the company is in adminstration;
- the Secretary of State has so directed; or
- the company is aligning its ARD with a subsidiary or parent under-taking in the EC.

The change must be made during a current period and details must be sent to the Registrar on Form 225. No time limit is specified but it must be sent before the end of the period.

FILING THE ACCOUNTS

Accounts must usually be filed 10 months after the ARD. If the company's first accounts cover a period of more than 12 months, however, they must be filed within 22 months of the date of incorporation. If the accounting reference period has been shortened the time allowed is 10 months or, if longer, three months from the date on Form 225.

For filing purposes a month after a specified date ends on the same date in the appropriate month, ie if the ARD is 30 October 2005, accounts must be filed before midnight on 30 August 2006. If there is no such date, eg the ARD ends on 30 April, accounts must be filed on the last day of the following February.

Extending the filing date

You can apply for a three-month extension:

- If you carry on business or have interests abroad. Form 244 must be delivered to Companies House before the normal filing deadline and filed for every year the company claims the extension.
- In special circumstances, eg if something beyond the company or the auditors' control delays the accounts. Written application must be made before the filing deadline, setting out the reasons for and the length of the required extension, to the Secretary of State for Trade and Industry. Companies incorporated in England and Wales apply c/o Companies Administration Section, Companies House, Cardiff. For Scottish companies the application is to Companies House, Edinburgh.

The *annual return* is sent to the Registrar on Form 363a (see page 93), signed by a director or the secretary. It must be made up to the 'return date', which is the anniversary of incorporation or, if the last return was made up to a different date, on the anniversary of that date.

STRIKING THE COMPANY OFF THE REGISTER

Failure to file returns or accounts may lead to an enquiry as to whether the company has ceased trading and the Registrar may delete the company from the Register if:

- up-to-date information about the company's activities has not been filed; or
- there are no effective officers; or
- mail sent to the registered office is returned undelivered; or
- information is received that the company has ceased trading.

Before taking action the Registrar writes to the company to make enquiries. Failing a response, he then informs the company, and publishes notice in the *Gazette*, of his intention to strike the company off after three months unless cause is shown to the contrary. Before striking off, the Registrar considers the objections of creditors and may delay taking action in order to allow them to pursue their claims and to petition to wind up the company. Notice of striking off will then be published in the *Gazette*. If there are assets they are *bona vacantia*, that is, they belong to the Crown, the Duchy of Lancaster or the Duchy of Cornwall, depending on the location of the registered office.

7

Insolvency

Limited liability means that if the business is insolvent, management's only liability is for fraud and for recklessness and incompetence which has jeopardised the interests of the creditors.

This chapter summarises the various procedures for winding up the company, but if drastic decisions must be made you should take expert advice. All the procedures require reference to, and action by, an insolvency practitioner, who must be a member of a recognised professional body such as the Institute of Chartered Accountants or the Law Society, or authorised by the Secretary of State. The procedures involve formalities, meetings of shareholders and creditors, time limits, reporting to and filing documentation with the Registrar, and publicity. There are fines and penalties if you do not comply with the statutory requirements.

WHAT IS INSOLVENCY?

A company is legally insolvent if it is unable to pay its debts and discharge its liabilities as and when they fall due, or the value of its assets is less than its liabilities. In determining liabilities, contingent and prospective liabilities must be taken into account, as well as actual and quantified amounts. Day-to-day involvement in management often gives a false picture of the company's financial position. If customers are slow to pay, plant, machinery and stock have been purchased under credit agreements and the company's bank account is in overdraft, the business may be far from healthy, however heavy the order book. Financial problems need not, however, lead to liquidation. The procedures introduced by the 1986 Insolvency Act permit a company to reach a compromise agreement with creditors, or to apply to the court for an administration order, so that company affairs can be reorganised and supervised and insolvency avoided.

You should therefore ensure that you have adequate accounting records and proper financial advice so that you are able to consider taking appropriate action.

VOLUNTARY STRIKING OFF

If a company has effectively ceased to operate, the Registrar may consider a written request to strike the company off the Register. If the company is struck off, any remaining assets pass to the Crown, the Duchy of Lancaster or the Duchy of Cornwall, depending on the location of the registered office. If there are debts, the creditors can object and, in any event, the directors', management's and shareholders' liability continues as if the company had not been dissolved.

VOLUNTARY ARRANGEMENTS: COMPOSITIONS AND SCHEMES OF ARRANGEMENT

Arrangements with creditors

These procedures offer a relatively straightforward method whereby a potentially solvent company concludes a legally effective arrangement with creditors with minimum reference to the court.

Procedure

The directors, or the liquidator or administrator (see below), put a statement of affairs – which sets out the company's financial position – and detailed proposals to creditors and shareholders for a scheme or composition in satisfaction of debts. They must nominate an insolvency practitioner to supervise the arrangement and, unless he or she is a liquidator or administrator, he or she must report to the court as to the necessity for shareholders' and creditors' meetings and notify creditors. A liquidator or administrator must call meetings but need not report to court. The meetings must approve the supervisor and can accept, modify or reject the proposals. Secured and preferred creditors are protected; directors, shareholders, creditors and the supervisor can challenge decisions and implementation.

The arrangement is carried out by the supervisor and he or she can refer to the court, which can stay (stop) the winding up and discharge an administration order.

ADMINISTRATION ORDERS

This procedure is mainly for companies which do not borrow on standard fixed and floating charges. It enables a potentially or actually insolvent company to put its affairs in the hands of an administrator, so that part or all of the company can be salvaged or a more advantageous realisation of assets can be secured than on a winding up.

Application is made to the court, which must be satisfied that the company is, or is likely to become, unable to pay its debts. In addition, the court must consider:

- that the order would be likely to enable part or all of the undertaking to survive as a going concern;
- and/or creditors are likely to agree a satisfactory arrangement with the company;
- and/or realisation of the assets is likely to be more advantageous than if the company were wound up.

The order can be used together with a voluntary arrangement or compromise or arrangement with creditors under the Companies Acts but not if the company is already in liquidation.

The petition is presented to the court by the company and/or directors and/or creditors and notice must be given to debenture-holders who have appointed, or have the right to appoint, an administrative receiver under a floating charge. On presentation of the petition, the administrator takes over management and no legal proceedings can issue or continue against the company, but an administrative receiver can be appointed and a petition for winding up can be presented. A more detailed statement of affairs verifed on affidavit by current and former officers of the company and, in some circumstances, employees, is drawn up. The administrator's proposals for reorganisation, which depend on the terms of the court order, can be rejected by shareholders, creditors or the court although the creditors' approval is not mandatory.

RECEIVERSHIP

This is the procedure by which assets secured by a floating charge are realised. Secured creditors can enforce their security independently of a winding up and without regard to the unsecured creditors or to the interests of the company.

Administrative receivers are appointed under a debenture secured by a charge and the appointment can be over all or a substantial part of the company's assets. The appointment can be by the debenture-holders or the court, and again the administrative receiver takes over management.

Receivers are appointed under the terms of a fixed charge or by the court but they cannot act as administrative receivers. Their powers depend on the terms of the charge or court order. The appointment suspends the fixed charge holders' right to enforce their security without the consent of the court or administrator, who can dispose of the charged property, giving them the same priority as they would have had if they had enforced the charge directly.

RECEIVERS AND DIRECTORS

The directors' powers effectively cease when a receiver or administrative receiver is appointed. A receiver ceases to act when he or she has sufficient funds to discharge the debt due to his or her appointor and his or her expenses but an administrative receiver can only be removed by court order.

VOLUNTARY ARRANGEMENT

There have been frequent complaints that secured creditors, particularly banks, act primarily in their own interests and ignore the interests of other creditors and the company.

With some exceptions appointing an administrative receiver has been barred under charges created on or after 20 June 2003. Instead, securities must be enforced through the appointment of an administrator who owes a duty and has to account to all the company's creditors.

The appointment can still be made by the court, but holders of a floating charge can on two days' notice, or the company or its directors on five days' notice, choose instead to file a notice of appointment with the court. No reports have to be filed explaining why the company should go into administration. However, the company or the directors (but not the floating charge-holder) must file a statement that the company is or is likely to become unable to pay its debts, and that the administrator believes that the purpose of administration is reasonably likely to be achieved.

The administrator then takes over management of the company to:

- rescue the company as a going concern; or
- achieve a better result for the creditors as a whole than would be likely if the company were wound up without first going into administration; or
- realise the assets in order to make a distribution to the secured or preferential creditors.

Time limits have been shortened and there is an overall time limit of one year for the process of administration, with an extension of six months with the creditors' consent or longer if the court so orders. If the administrator is unable to rescue the company, he or she must file a notice with the court converting to a creditors' voluntary liquidation and he or she acts as liquidator unless the creditors decide otherwise.

PROTECTION FOR FLOATING CHARGE-HOLDERS

The floating charge-holder can choose his or her own administrator even if there is already an application before the court, unless the court decides otherwise and can also apply for the appointment of an administrator if the company is in compulsory liquidation.

VOLUNTARY ARRANGEMENT WITH A MORATORIUM

This scheme requires proposals for a voluntary arrangement being put to the company by a nominated insolvency practitioner, who calls shareholders' and creditors' meetings to approve the voluntary arrangement and on approval supervises the arrangement. When the proposals are drawn up and supported by the nominee the directors can obtain a 28-day moratorium (which stops creditors and others from enforcing their legal remedies) by filing the terms of the proposals and certain other documents with the court. There must be both creditors' and shareholders' meetings, the moratorium must be advertised and the registrar notified. The 28-day period can be shortened and, with the creditors' consent, extended by two months.

During the moratorium the nominee monitors the company's affairs and the directors cannot act without his or her consent. The moratorium ends with the calling of the required meetings that either approve or reject the voluntary arrangement. If there is disagreement, the decision of the creditors' meeting is decisive.

Procedurally this is more complicated and public than a voluntary arrangement. There are more constraints on the directors and it is likely to be more costly because of the increased involvement of the insolvency practitioner.

WINDING UP

This is the statutory procedure which brings a company's operations to an end, realising the assets and distributing the proceeds among creditors and shareholders in accordance with their rights. The company is then dissolved.

A company can be wound up compulsorily by court order or voluntarily by the shareholders if it is insolvent, or by shareholders if it is solvent.

VOLUNTARY WINDING UP

The company puts itself into voluntary liquidation by passing a resolution at a general meeting of the shareholders. Seven days' notice of the meeting must be given and a notice of a creditors' meeting to be held on the same day or the day after must be sent on the same date. The decision can be by ordinary resolution if the company was formed for a fixed period or a specific undertaking; otherwise a special resolution must be passed. An extraordinary resolution is necessary if the company is insolvent.

VOLUNTARY LIQUIDATION

A members' or shareholders' voluntary liquidation requires the majority of the directors to prepare a declaration of solvency after full enquiry into the company's affairs. The declaration sets out the company's assets and liabilities and states that it will be able to pay its debts within, at most, 12 months; if they are not paid, the directors may be liable to a fine or imprisonment.

If no declaration is made or the liquidator disagrees with its conclusion or the company cannot pay its debts within 12 months, it becomes a creditors' voluntary liquidation and the creditors appoint and can supervise the liquidator.

The advantage of a voluntary liquidation is that, although employees are dismissed if the company is insolvent, the directors can continue to act provided they have the approval of the liquidator and of the shareholders given in general meeting. In a creditors' voluntary liquidation the creditors must also give their consent.

If the resolution is passed without appointing a liquidator, the directors can dispose of perishable goods and those likely to diminish in value unless immediately disposed of, and take action necessary to protect company assets until one is appointed. Any further action requires the consent of the court, and the company must stop trading except in so far as may be required for beneficial winding up.

The liquidation starts on the date the resolution for winding up is passed; if the liquidator thinks the company is insolvent, the winding up continues as a creditors' voluntary liquidation. The liquidator stays in office until removed after his or her final report to shareholders and creditors but he or she can resign or vacate office on notice to the Registrar of the final meeting.

DISTRIBUTION

Available assets are applied against the company's liabilities, and shareholders are only called on for any balance remaining unpaid on their shares.

CREDITORS' RIGHTS

Fixed charge-holders take the first slice of the assets, followed by liquidation expenses, preferential debts, floating chargeholders and sums due to shareholders (for instance, arrears of dividend). In some circumstances floating charge-holders may have prior claims to holders of a fixed charge. Remaining assets go to unsecured creditors, who can claim interest to the date of distribution, and any surplus is divided among shareholders in accordance with their rights under the Memorandum and Articles of Association.

Preferential debts comprise:

- outstanding tax to a maximum of 12 months, including PAYE;
- contributions in respect of subcontractors in the construction industry;
- six months' VAT;
- general betting duty;
- 12 months' National Insurance contributions;
- state and occupational pension scheme contributions;
- arrears of wages for four months (including directors but not the managing director) to a maximum of £240 per week, including Statutory Sick Pay, protective awards, payment during medical suspension, time off work and accrued holiday pay.

Wages Act employee claims are paid if the company has more than 10 employees. Most amounts payable to employees under the employment legislation can be reimbursed partly or wholly from the Redundancy Fund. Employees can claim for any balance still outstanding with the ordinary (unsecured) creditors.

DISSOLUTION IN A VOLUNTARY LIQUIDATION

The company is dissolved three months from registration by the Registrar of the liquidator's final account and return.

COMPULSORY WINDING UP

The compulsory procedure can be initiated by the company, a share-holder, a creditor, the official receiver (employed by the Department of Trade and Industry), or the Department of Trade and Industry.

The most frequent basis for the petition is insolvency, which here is presumed if a creditor has been owed at least £750 for more than three weeks after a formal demand has been served, or the company has not discharged a judgement debt or court order. The court appoints a liquidator who can, without reference to the court or creditors, take over management of the company forthwith. Here the liquidator not only gets in and distributes the assets but also must provide the official receiver with any information and documents he or she requires. The official receiver must look into the cause of the company's failure, reporting if necessary to the court, and he or she can apply for public examination of officers, liquidators, administrators and anyone else involved in the company's affairs.

FINES AND PENALTIES

If the company has been trading with an intent to defraud creditors or anyone else, or incurring debts without a reasonable prospect of repayment, anyone involved may be prosecuted and disqualified from participating directly or indirectly in the management of a company for a maximum of 15 years. Conviction for an indictable offence (that is, a serious offence triable by jury in the Crown Court) relating to the promotion, formation, management or liquidation of a company, or with the receivership or management of its property, or for persistent failure to file accounts and records, can also lead to disqualification.

Fraudulent and wrongful trading can in addition bring a personal liability for all the company's debts. Fraudulent trading is trading with an intent to defraud creditors. If the company is in insolvent liquidation and a director, *de facto*, or shadow director knew, or should have known, that there was no reasonable prospect that the company could have avoided insolvent liquidation, there may also be criminal liability for wrongful trading and disqualification.

Officers of the company and anyone else acting in the promotion, formation, management or liquidation of a company in liquidation are personally liable if they retain or misapply assets or they are in breach of duty to the company.

VOIDABLE TRANSACTIONS: PREFERENCES AND TRANSACTIONS AT AN UNDERVALUE

Any transaction entered into by an insolvent company which puts a creditor, surety or guarantor into a better position than he or she would be in the liquidation may be voidable and set aside as a (fraudulent) 'preference'. The preference may be a transaction at a proper price or at an undervalue (that is, a gratuitous gift or transfer or one made for significantly less than market value). The risk period dates back from presentation of a petition for an administrative order or the date the order is made, or the commencement of liquidation.

Transactions at a proper price or an undervalue are safe if made in good faith and for the purpose of carrying on the business, provided that at the time there were reasonable grounds that the transaction would benefit the company. They are at risk, however, if made at a time when the company was unable to pay its debts or it became unable to pay them as a result of the transaction. Preferences at an undervalue and any preference, even one at a proper price, with a connected person is at risk for two years. There is a six-month risk period for other preferences and preferences made in the period prior to the making of an administration order.

The network of connected persons here extends further and includes:

- directors;
- shadow directors, ie persons in accordance with whose instructions directors are accustomed to act;
- company officers and their spouses, including former and reputed spouses;
- their children and step-children;
- their partners;
- companies with which they are associated;
- companies of which they control at least one-fifth of the voting shares;
- trustees of any trust under which they, their family group, or associated company is a beneficiary

Floating charges may also be voidable. They are valid whenever created to the extent that consideration (that is, payment in cash, goods or services or in discharge of debts) is received by the company. The balance is at risk for one year if made when the company was unable to pay its debts, and two years if made in favour of a connected person.

Distribution is on the same basis as in voluntary liquidation.

DISSOLUTION IN COMPULSORY WINDING UP

The liquidator reports to a final meeting of creditors when winding up is completed. If the official receiver is acting, he or she can apply for early dissolution on the basis that assets will not cover winding up expenses and no further investigation is required. Three months from the date of registration of dissolution entered by the Registrar, the company is dissolved.

RESTRICTION ON USE OF THE COMPANY NAME

Directors and shadow directors acting within 12 months of insolvent liquidation cannot act for, or be involved with, a company with the same name. Nor can they for five years use a former name or trading name used during the previous 12 months or one so similar as to suggest continuing association, without the consent of the court. Non-compliance brings a personal joint and several liability with the company and anyone acting on the offender's instructions.

8

The ready-made company

The fastest way to incorporation is to buy an 'off the shelf', ready-made company already registered at Companies House from your solicitor or accountant or one of the many registration agents who advertise in financial and professional journals and the *Yellow Pages*. All the necessary documentation will have been filed with the Registrar and the company will have a Certificate of Incorporation, so that it can start trading as soon as you have appointed your own director(s) and secretary and transferred the shares to your own shareholders.

Your solicitor or accountant can incorporate your company through a company agent's fast-track electronic filing service for as little as £19.99. If you want to choose your own company name they will check its availability for a fee. If you intend to use the name as a trade mark, you should also carry out a search at the Trade Marks Registry in the appropriate class of goods and services.

Companies House will send you information packs and guides and agents will advise you on the necessary initial changes for takeover. The objects clause can be changed but you should ensure that the existing principal objects clause covers your main business activities.

You will then have a company with a current Certificate of Incorporation, a standard Memorandum of Association with an appropriate objects and capital clause, standard Articles of Association, a set of statutory books and a company seal if this is required by your Articles. The existing directors, secretary and shareholders of the ready-made company, usually the agent's nominees, resign in favour of your nominees.

If the nominee shareholders were companies, your ready-made company cannot claim exemption from audit for its accounts (see page 100), unless it is dormant throughout its first financial year. It may therefore be worthwhile shortening the first accounting period so it ends on the day on which you take ownership of the shares (see page 92). The company must, however, pass a special resolution not to appoint auditors and deliver dormant company accounts for the first (shortened) period, before the first general meeting at which accounts are laid.

You may wish to make other changes, which must be notified to the Registrar of Companies in accordance with the Companies Act, and which are dealt with in Chapter 6. These involve some delay but the procedure is more straightforward and less expensive than starting from scratch.

Appendix 1

NOTES FOR GUIDANCE ON COMPANY NAMES

A. Use of the following words and expressions in a company or business name requires the prior approval of the Secretary of State for Trade and Industry:

(a) *Words that imply national or international pre-eminence*

International	British	Wales
National	England	Welsh
European	English	Ireland
United Kingdom	Scotland	Irish
Great Britain	Scottish	

(b) *Words that imply business pre-eminence or representative or authoritative status*

Association	Authority	Board
Council	Federation	Institute
Institution	Society	

(c) *Words that imply specific objects or functions*

Assurance	Reinsurance,	Chemist
Insurance	Reassurance	Chemistry
Trade Union	Insurer	Group
Foundation	Assurer	Holding
Fund	Reassurer	Post Office

Charity
Charter
Chartered
Cooperative
Stock Exchange
Trust
Benevolent
Sheffield

Reinsurer
Patent
Patentee
Chamber of Trade

Register
Registered
Friendly Society

B. Use of the following words and expressions also requires the prior consent of the relevant body as well as the Secretary of State. A statement that a written request has been made to the relevant body seeking its opinion as to use of the word or expression must be filed with the application for registration, together with a copy of any response:

Word or expression	Relevant body for persons intending to to set up business in England or Wales	Relevant body for persons intending to to set up business Scotland
Royale, Royale Royalty, King, Queen, Prince, Princess, Windsor, Duke, His/Her Majesty	Grant Bavister Department Constitutional Affairs 6th Floor Selbourne House 54 Victoria Street London SW1E 6QW (if based in England) The National Assembly for Wales Crown Buildings Cathays Park Cardiff CF1 3NQ (if based in Wales)	The Scottish Minister Civil Law and LA Division Saughton House Broomhouse Drive Edinburgh EH11 3XD
Police	Home Office Police Dept Strategy Group Room 510 50 Queen Anne's Gate London SW1H 9AT	The Scottish Minister's Police Division 50 Andrew's House Regent Road Edinburgh EH1 3DQ

Special School	Department for Education and Employment Schools 2 Branch Sanctuary Buildings Gt Smith St London SW1P 3BT	As for England & Wales
Contact Lens	General Optical Council 41 Wimpole Street, London W1N 2DJ	As for England & Wales
District Nurse, Health Visitor, Midwife, Midwifery, Health Visiting, Nurse, Nursing	The Registrar and Chief Executive United Kingdom Central Council for Nursing and Midwifery 23 Portland Place London W1N 3AF	As for England & Wales
Health Centre	Office of the Solicitor Department of Health and Social Security 48 Carey Street London WC2A 2LS	As for England & Wales
Health Service	Department of Health, NHS Management Wellington House 133–135 Waterloo Road London SE1 8UG	As for England & Wales
Pregnancy, Termination, Abortion	Department of Health, Room 2N35A Quarry House Quarry Hill Leeds LS2 7UE	As for England & Wales

Charity, Charitable	Head of Status Charity Commission Registration Division Woodfield Tangier House Taunton TA1 4BL	Scotland: Inland Revenue FICO (Scotland) Trinity Park House South Trinity Road Edinburgh EH5 3SD
Apothecary	The Worshipful Society of Apothecaries of London Apothecaries Hall Blackfriars Lane London EC4V 6EJ	The Pharmaceutical Society of Great Britain Law Department 1 Lambeth High Street London SE1 7JN
University	Privy Council Office 2 Carlton Gardens London SW1Y 5AA	As for England & Wales

C. The use of certain words is covered by other legislation and may constitute a criminal offence. Some of these words are listed below but the list is not exhaustive. If you wish to use any of them, you should seek legal advice and confirmation from the body concerned that the use of the word does not contravene the relevant legislation, but their opinion is not conclusive:

Word or expression	*Relevant legislation*	*Relevant body*
Architect	Section 20 Architects Registration Registration Act 1997	Architects Registration Board 73 Hallan Street London W1N 6EE
Chiropodist, Dietician, Medical Laboratory, Technician, Occupational Therapist, Orthoptist, Physiotherapist, Radiographer, Remedial Gymnast, professions supplementary to	Medicine Act 1960	Department of Health Room 2N35A HRD HRB Quarry House Quarry Hill Leeds LS2 7JE

Medicine Act 1960
if preceded by
Registered, State or State
Registered

Credit Union	Credit Union Act 1979	The Registrar of Friendly Societies 25 North Colonnade Canary Wharf London E14 5HS
		Scottish Association Associate Registrar of Friendly Societies 58 Frederick St Edinburgh EH2 1NB
Dentist, Dental Surgeon, Dental Practitioner, Dentistry	Dental Act 1984	The Registrar General Dental Council 37 Wimpole St London W1M 8DQ
Veterinary Surgeon, Veterinary, Vet	Sections 19/20 Veterinary Surgeons Act 1966	The Registrar Royal College of Veterinary Surgeons Belgravia House 62–64 Horseferry Road London SW1P 2AF
Optician, ophthalmic optician, dispensing optician, enrolled optician, registered optician, optometrist	Opticians Act 1989	The Registrar General Optical Council 41 Harley Street London W1N 2DJ

Solicitor (Scotland)	Act of Scotland 1980	The Law Society of Scotland 26 Drumsheugh Gardens Edinburgh EH3 7HR
Pharmaceutical Druggist, Pharmaceutical Pharmaceutist, Pharmacist, Pharmacy	Section 78 Medicines Act 1968	The Director of Legal Services The Royal Pharmaceutical Society of Great Britain 1 Lambeth High St London SE1 7JN Scotland: The Pharmaceutical Society 36 York Place Edinburgh EH13 3HU
Red Cross, Geneva Cross, Red Crescent, Red Lion and Sun	Geneva Convention Act 1957	Seek advice of Companies House
Anzac	Anzac Act 1916	Seek advice of Companies House
Inst of Laryngology, Inst of Otology, Inst of Urology, Inst of Orthopaedics	University College of London Act 1988	Seek advice of University College Gower Street London WC1E 6BT
Olympiad, Olympiads, Olympian, Olympians, Olympic, Olympics, or translation of these	Olympic Symbol etc (Protection) Act 1995*	British Olympic Association 1 Wandsworth Plain London SW18 1EH

*Also protects Olympic symbols of five interlocking rings and motto *'Citius Altius Fortius'*

Patent Office, Patent Agent	Copyright Design & Patents Act 1988	IPDD, Room 3B38 Concept House The Patent Office Cardiff Road Newport NP10 8QQ
Building Society and Friendly Society	Building Society Act 1986 Friendly Society Act 1874	The Registry of Friendly Societies 25 The North Colonnade Canary Wharf London E14 5HS
Chamber(s) of Business, Chamber(s) of Commerce, Chamber(s) of Commerce & Industry, Chamber(s) of Commerce, Training & Enterprise Chamber(s) of Enterprise Chamber(s) of Industry Chamber(s) of Trade Chamber(s) of Trade and Industry, Chamber(s) of Training Chamber(s) of Training and Enterprise or Welsh translations of these words	Company & Business Names (Chamber of Commerce etc) Act 1999	Guidance available from Companies House

Only persons carrying on business as a building society in the UK may use a name which implies that they are in any way connected with the business of a building society.

D. 'Too like' names – The Secretary of State takes account of facts which might suggest similarity and lead to confusion including, for instance, the nature and location of a business. Evidence to show confusion is taken into account.

E. A name suggesting a connection with a company already on the Index – The Secretary of State does not consider 'implied association' – ie whether the company might be thought to be a member of, or associated with, another company or group. Nor is consideration given to trading names, logos, trade or service marks, copyrights, patents, etc or any other proprietary rights existing in names or parts of names.

F.   Company letterhead – Business owned by a company:

Bert's Shoes

6 Tuppeny Passage, London NW12 5TT

Bert's Shoes (UK) Limited
Registered in England and Wales
Registration Number: 123456789
Registered Office, 81 Florin Way, London NW13 7DD

The restrictions applying to business names are similar to those applying to company names.

Information required to be disclosed by the Business Names Act 1985 and the Companies Act 1985.

Appendix 2

DOCUMENTS TO BE FILED ON INCORPORATION BY A PRIVATE LIMITED LIABILITY COMPANY

1. MEMORANDUM OF ASSOCIATION, stating the company's name, the situation of its registered office (England, Scotland or Wales), the objects for which the company is formed and the powers taken by the company, that the liability of the shareholders is limited and the amount of the share capital divided into shares of a fixed amount. It must be dated and subscribed by not less than two persons (the subscribers), their signatures duly witnessed.

2. ARTICLES OF ASSOCIATION (unless Table A (see page 20) is adopted), setting out the regulations governing the company's internal affairs. This must be printed, dated and signed by the subscribers to the Memorandum and their signatures duly witnessed.

3. Statement of First Directors and Secretary and Intended Situation of Registered Office (Form 10). The form can be signed by the subscribers to the Memorandum or by agents acting on their behalf and sets out the prescribed details of the directors and secretary, who must also sign the form confirming their consent to act.

4. Declaration of Compliance with the Requirements on Application for Registration of a Company (Form 12). This can be made by a director or secretary named in the Statement of first officers above or by a solicitor engaged in the company's formation.

Appendix 3

DOCUMENTS WHICH MUST BE LODGED WITH THE REGISTRAR*

Document	Form	Signatories	When lodged	Penalty
Statement of first directors secretary and intended situation of registered office	10	Subscribers or their agent and each officer	Before registration	None
Declaration of compliance with requirements on application for registration	12	Director, secretary or solicitor acting	ditto	None
Notice of change of registered office	287	Director or secretary	Within 14 days of change	£400 + £40 daily
Notice of change directors, secretary or in their particulars	288	ditto	ditto	£2,000 + £200 daily

Document	Form	Signatories	When lodged	Penalty
Contract constituting allottees' title to shares and contract of sale	–	All parties to contract	Within 14 days of change	£2,000 + £200 daily
Particulars of contract re shares allotted as fully or partly paid up otherwise than in cash	88(3)	Director or secretary	Within 1 month of allotment of shares for non-cash consideration (used when no written contract)	ditto
Return of allotment of shares	88(2)	ditto	Within 1 month of allotment	No limit on indictment. £2,000 on summary conviction + £200 daily
(first) Notice of accounting reference date	224	ditto	Within 9 months of incorporation	None but date is then 31/3
Notice of new accounting reference date	225	ditto	Before end of period	None but change ineffective
Accounts	225	Director	Within 10 months of accounting reference period	£100 to £1,000 depending on delay

* The documentation listed covers the more straightforward company business. It does not include documentation which must be filed when you are involved in transactions requiring specialist legal and/or accountancy advice, for instance where application has been made to the court to vary shareholders' rights or to reduce the company's share capital.

Annual return	363a	Director or secretary	Within 28 days of the return date	£2,000 + £200 daily
Special resolution	–	Director, secretary or chairman of meeting	Within 15 days of passing resolution	£1,000 + £40 daily
Extraordinary resolution	–	Director, secretary or chairman of meeting	Within 15 days of passing resolution	£400 + £40 daily
Other resolution or agreement by all members or class of members not otherwise effective unless passed as special or extraordinary resolution	–	ditto	ditto	ditto
Resolution authorising increase of share capital	–	ditto	ditto	ditto
Notice of increase in nominal capital	123	Director or secretary	ditto	ditto
Notice of passing of resolution removing an auditor	386	ditto	Within 14 days of passing resolution	ditto
Notice of place where copies of director's service contracts kept or of change in place	318	ditto	Within 14 days	ditto

Document	Form	Signatories	When lodged	Penalty
Notice of place where register of members kept or of change in place	353	ditto	ditto	ditto
Notice of place where register of holders of debentures or duplicate kept or of change in place	190	ditto	Not specified	Not specified
Notice of place where register of directors' interests in shares, etc, kept or of change in place	325	Director or secretary	Within 14 days daily	£400 + £40 daily
Particulars of mortgage or charge	395	Director, secretary, solicitor to company or mortgagee	Within 21 days of creation (instrument also to be produced)	No limit on conviction on indictment. £2,000 on summary conviction + £200 daily
Particulars for registration of charge to secure series of debentures	397	Director, secretary, solicitor to company or debenture holder or their solicitor	Within 21 days of execution of trust deed or debentures (if no deed) and the deed or one debenture	ditto
Particulars of a mortgage or charge subject to which property has been acquired	400	Director or secretary	Within 21 days of acquisition	ditto

Declaration of satisfaction in full or in part of mortgage or charge	403a	Under company seal at company's option but best attested as required by articles	lodged forthwith	ditto
Declaration that part of property or undertaking (a) has been released from charge; (b) no longer forms part of undertaking	403b	Under company seal attested as required by articles	At company's option but best lodged forthwith	No limit on conviction on indictment. £2,000 on summary conviction + £200 daily.
Notice of appointment receiver or manager	405(1)*	Person obtaining order or making appointment or their solicitor	Within 7 days of court order or appointment	£400 + £40 daily
Notice of ceasing to act as receiver or manager	405(2)*	Receiver or manager	On ceasing to act	ditto
Printed copy of memorandum as altered by special resolution	–	–	Within 15 days after period for making application to court for cancelling alteration	ditto

*Not illustrated

Note: Documents sent to Companies House are microfilmed; forms should therefore be completed legibly and in black ink. Typed documents should be on A4 paper with a margin of not less than 10 millimetres (20 millimetres if documents are bound). Computer print is acceptable but dot matrix and carbon copy documents are not.

Accompanying cheques should be made payable to Companies House.

Fees for inspection, copies and extracts
Companies House provides public records of information filed by companies on paper, microfiche, roll film and magnetic tape and via e-mail, fax (ordered by credit/debit card) and courier as well as via database direct to your PC. Credit card customers and account holders can only order by telephone, and credit card orders are subject to a minimum charge of £5.

The following company details are available free of charge on the Companies House website at www.companieshouse.gov.uk:

- company indexes;
- basic company details;
- a history of company transactions;
- the register of disqualified directors;
- insolvency details.

There is no charge for viewing some company documents online; others can be viewed for a charge of £1–£4, and they can be downloaded for £2.00. Payment is by credit card with a minimum charge of £5.00.

The charge for a paper copy ordered by post or telephone is £3; a faxed copy costs £12.

Companies House also provides bulk compilations, including company analysis listed by VAT trade classification, postcode, incorporation date or company status and a Register of Directors, Register of Registered Charges and New Incorporation Prints. More detailed analysis of the information held by Companies House is available on request.

High volume users, for instance, company formation agents, can use the electronic incorporation service but otherwise filing is by post, Document Exchange or courier. Faxed copies of statutory documents are not accepted for registration. Acknowledgement of receipt of documents is only given if postage or carriage is pre-paid.

Enquiries can be made by e-mail to enquiries@companieshjouse.gov.uk and by telephone to 0870 333 3636 or fax to 02920 380517.

COMPANIES FORM No. 128(1)

G

Statement of rights attached to allotted shares

128(1)

CHW P000

Please do not write in this margin

Pursuant to section 128(1) of the Companies Act 1985

Please complete legibly, preferably in black type, or bold block lettering

To the Registrar of Companies
(Address overleaf)

For official use   Company number

Name of company

* insert full name of company

has allotted shares with rights which:

i. are not stated in the company's memorandum or articles or in any resolution or agreement to which section 380 of the above Act applies, and

ii. are not in all respects uniform with those attached to shares previously allotted.

† delete as appropriate

The class[es]† of such shares and the date of the first allotment of shares in each class and the rights attached to each class are:

Class of Shares	Date of first allotment

Description of Rights

‡ Insert Director, Secretary, Administrator, Administrative Receiver or Receiver (Scotland) as appropriate

Signed   Designation‡   Date

Presenter's name address and reference (if any) :

For official Use   (02/06)
General Section   Post room

Figure A3.1 Statement of rights attached to allotted shares

G

COMPANIES FORM No. 128(3)

Statement of particulars of variation of rights attached to shares

128(3)

CHW P000

Please do not write in this margin

Pursuant to section 128(3) of the Companies Act 1985

Please complete legibly, preferably in black type, or bold block lettering

To the Registrar of Companies
(Address overleaf)

For official use

Company number

Name of company

* insert full name of company

*

† insert date

On † _____ the rights attached to

Number of Shares	Class(es) of share

were varied as set out below (otherwise than by amendment of the company's memorandum or articles or by any resolution or agreement to which section 380 of the above Act applies)

‡ Insert Director, Secretary, Administrator, Administrative Receiver or Receiver (Scotland) as appropriate

Signed

Designation‡

Date

Presenter's name address and reference (if any) :

For official Use (02/06)
General Section

Post room

Figure A3.2 Statement of particulars of variation of rights attached to shares

Notes

The address for companies registered in England and Wales or Wales is :-

The Registrar of Companies
Companies House
Crown Way
Cardiff
CF14 3UZ

or, for companies registered in Scotland :-

The Registrar of Companies
Companies House
37 Castle Terrace
Edinburgh
EH1 2EB

Figure A3.2 *continued*

G

COMPANIES FORM No. 128(4)

Notice of assignment of name or new name to any class of shares

128(4)

CHW P000

Please do not write in this margin

Pursuant to section 128(4) of the Companies Act 1985

Please complete legibly, preferably in black type, or bold block lettering

To the Registrar of Companies
(Address overleaf)

For official use   Company number

Name of company

* insert full name of company

*

gives notice of the assignment of a [new]† name or other designation to the following class[es]† of shares (otherwise than by amendment of the company's memorandum or articles or by any resolution or agreement to which section 380 of the above Act applies)

† delete as appropriate

Number and class of shares	Name or other designation

‡ Insert Director, Secretary, Administrator, Administrative Receiver or Receiver (Scotland) as appropriate

Signed   Designation‡   Date

Presenter's name address and reference (if any) :

For official Use (02/06)
General Section   Post room

Figure A3.3   Notice of assignment of name or new name to any class of shares

Notes

The address for companies registered in England and Wales or Wales is :-

The Registrar of Companies
Companies House
Crown Way
Cardiff
CF14 3UZ

or, for companies registered in Scotland :-

The Registrar of Companies
Companies House
37 Castle Terrace
Edinburgh
EH1 2EB

Figure A3.3 *continued*

G

CHWP000

COMPANIES FORM No. 155(6)(a)

Declaration in relation to assistance for the acquisition of shares

155(6)a

Please do not write in this margin

Pursuant to section 155(6) of the Companies Act 1985

Please complete legibly, preferably in black type, or bold block lettering

To the Registrar of Companies **(Address overleaf - Note 5)**

For official use   Company number

Name of company

Note
Please read the notes on page 3 before completing this form.

*

* insert full name of company

I/We ø

ø insert name(s) and address(es) of all the directors

† delete as appropriate

[the sole director][all the directors]† of the above company do solemnly and sincerely declare that:

The business of the company is:

§ delete whichever is inappropriate

(a) that of a [recognised bank][licensed institution]† within the meaning of the Banking Act 1979§

(b) that of a person authorised under section 3 or 4 of the Insurance Companies Act 1982 to carry on insurance business in the United Kingdom§

(c) something other than the above§

The company is proposing to give financial assistance in connection with the acquisition of shares in the [company] [company's holding company _____

_____ Limited]†

The assistance is for the purpose of [that acquisition][reducing or discharging a liability incurred for the purpose of that acquisition].†

The number and class of the shares acquired or to be acquired is: _____

_____

Presenter's name address and reference (if any) :

For official Use (02/06)
General Section   Post room

Page 1

Figure A3.4   Declaration in relation to assistance for the acquisition of shares

The assistance is to be given to: (note 2) _____

_____

_____

_____

The assistance will take the form of:

The person who [has acquired][will acquire]† the share is:

_____

_____

The principal terms on which the assistance will be given are:

The amount of cash to be transferred to the person assisted is £ _____

The value of any asset to be transferred to the person assisted is £ _____

The date on which the assistance is to be given is _____

Page 2

Figure A3.4 *continued*

I/We have formed the opinion, as regards the company's initial situation immediately following the date on which the assistance is proposed to be given, that there will be no ground on which it could then be found to be unable to pay its debts. (note 3)

(a) [I/We have formed the opinion that the company will be able to pay its debts as they fall due during the year immediately following that date]* (note 3)

(b) [It is intended to commence the winding-up of the company within 12 months of that date, and I/we have formed the opinion that the company will be able to pay its debts in full within 12 months of the commencement of the winding up.]* (note 3)

And I/we make this solemn declaration conscientiously believing the same to be true and by virtue of the provisions of the Statutory Declarations Act 1835.

Declared at _____   Declarants to sign below

_____

_____

Day　Month　Year

on [　|　|　|　|　|　|　|　]

before me _____

A Commissioner for Oaths or Notary Public or Justice of the Peace or a Solicitor having the powers conferred on a Commissioner for Oaths.

NOTES

1　For the meaning of "a person incurring a liability" and "reducing or discharging a liability" see section 152(3) of the Companies Act 1985.

2　Insert full name(s) and address(es) of the person(s) to whom assistance is to be given; if a recipient is a company the registered office address should be shown.

3　Contingent and prospective liabilities of the company are to be taken into account - see section 156(3) of the Companies Act 1985.

4　The auditors report required by section 156(4) of the Companies Act 1985 must be annexed to this form.

5　The address for companies registered in England and Wales or Wales is:-

The Registrar of Companies
Companies House
Crown Way
Cardiff
CF14 3UZ

DX 33050 Cardiff

or, for companies registered in Scotland:-

The Registrar of Companies
37 Castle Terrace
Edinburgh
EH1 2EB

DX 235 Edinburgh

or LP-4 Edinburgh 2

Page 3

Figure A3.4　*continued*

G

CHWP000

COMPANIES FORM No. 169

Return by a company purchasing its own shares

169

Please do not write in this margin

Pursuant to section 169 of the Companies Act 1985

Please do not write in the space below. For Inland Revenue use only.

Please complete legibly, preferably in black type, or bold block lettering

To the Registrar of Companies **(Address overleaf)**

For official use

Company number

Name of company

* insert full name of company

*

Note
This return must be delivered to the Registrar within a period of 28 days beginning with the first date on which shares to which it relates were delivered to the company

Shares were purchased by the company under section 162 of the above Act as follows:

Class of shares			
Number of shares purchased			
Nominal value of each share			
Date(s) on which the shares were delivered to the company			
Maximum prices paid § for each share			
Minimum prices paid § for each share			

§ A private company is not required to give this information

The aggregate amount paid by the company for the shares to which this return relates was:	£
Stamp Duty is payable on the aggregate amount at the rate of ¹/₂% rounded up to the nearest multiple of £5	£

‡ Insert Director, Secretary, Administrator, Administrative Receiver or Receiver (Scotland) as appropriate

Signed   Designation ‡   Date

Presenter's name address and reference (if any) :

For official Use (02/06)
General Section   Post room

Figure A3.5 Return by a company purchasing its own shares

1. Before this form is delivered to Companies House it must be "stamped" by the Inland Revenue Stamp Office to confirm that the appropriate amount of Stamp Duty has been paid. The Inland Revenue Stamp Offices is located at:

> London Stamp Office
> Ground Floor
> South West Wing
> Bush House
> Strand
> London
> WC2B 4QN
>
> Tel: 020 7438 7252/7452

Cheques for Stamp Duty must be made payable to "Inland Revenue - Stamp Duties" and crossed "Not Transferable".

NOTE. This form must be presented to the Inland Revenue Stamp Office for stamping together with the payment of duty within 30 days of the purchase of the shares, otherwise Inland Revenue penalties may be incurred.

2. After this form has been "stamped" and returned to you by the Inland Revenue it must be sent to:

> For companies registered in:

England or Wales:

> The Registrar of Companies
> Companies House
> Crown Way
> Cardiff CF14 3UZ
>
> DX: 33050 Cardiff

Scotland:

> The Registrar of Companies
> Companies House
> 37 Castle Terrace
> Edinburgh EH1 2EB
>
> DX: 235 Edinburgh
>
> or LP - 4 Edinburgh 2

Figure A3.5 *continued*

G

CHWP000

COMPANIES FORM No. 173

Declaration in relation to the redemption or purchase of shares out of capital

173

Please do not write in this margin

Pursuant to section 173 of the Companies Act 1985

Please complete legibly, preferably in black type, or bold block lettering

To the Registrar of Companies
(Address overleaf - Note 4)

For official use

Company number

Name of company

* insert full name of company

*

Note
Please read the notes on page 2 before completing this form.

ø insert name(s) and address(es) of all the directors

I / We ø

† delete as appropriate

[the sole director][all the directors]† of the above company do solemnly and sincerely declare that:

The business of the company is:

§ delete whichever is inappropriate

(a) that of a [recognised bank][licensed institution]† within the meaning of the Banking Act 1979§

(b) that of a person authorised under section 3 or 4 of the Insurance Companies Act 1982 to carry on insurance business in the United Kingdom§

(c) that of something other than the above§

The company is proposing to make a payment out of capital for the redemption or purchase of its own shares

The amount of the permissible capital payment for the shares in question is £_____ (note 1)

Continued overleaf

Presenter's name address and reference (if any) :

For official Use (02/06)
General Section

Post room

Page 1

Figure A3.6 Declaration of satisfaction in full or in part of mortgage or charge

I / We have made full enquiry into the affairs and prospects of the company, and I / we have formed the opinion:

(a) as regards its initial situation immediately following the date on which the payment out of capital is proposed to be made, that there will be no grounds on which the company could then be found unable to pay its debts (note 2), and

(b) as regards its prospects for the year immediately following that date, that, having regard to my/our intentions with respect to the management of the company's business during that year and to the amount and character of the financial resources which will in my / our view be available during that year, the company will be able to continue to carry on business as a going concern (and will accordingly be able to pay its debts as they fall due) throughout that year. (note 2)

And I / we make this solemn declaration conscientiously believing the same to be true and by virtue of the provisions of the Statutory Declarations Act 1835.

Declared at _____

Declarant(s) to sign below

Day	Month	Year

on

before me _____

A Commissioner for Oaths, or Notary Public, or Justice of the Peace, or Solicitor having the powers conferred on a Commissioner for Oaths.

Notes

1 'Permissible capital payment' means an amount which, taken together with
(i) any available profits of the company; and
(ii) the proceeds of any fresh issue of shares made for the purposes of the redemption or purchase;
Is equal to the price of redemption or purchase.
'Available profits' means the company's profits which are available for distribution (within the meaning of section 172 and 263 of the Companies Act 1985).
The question whether the company has any profits so available and the amount of any such profits is to be determined in accordance with section 172 of the Companies Act 1985.

2 Contingent and prospective liabilities of the company must be taken into account, see sections 173(4) & 517 of the Companies Act 1985.

3 A copy of this declaration together with a copy of the auditors report required by section 173 of the Companies Act 1985, must be delivered to the Registrar of Companies not later than the day on which the company publishes the notice required by section 175(1) of the Companies Act 1985, or first publishes or gives the notice required by section 175(2), whichever is the earlier.

4 The address for companies registered in England and Wales or Wales is:-

The Registrar of Companies
Companies House
Crown Way
Cardiff
CF14 3UZ

DX 33050 Cardiff

or, for companies registered in Scotland:-

The Registrar of Companies
Companies House
37 Castle Terrace
Edinburgh
EH1 2EB

DX 235 Edinburgh
or LP-4 Edinburgh 2

Page 2

Figure A3.6 *continued*

Companies House
— for the record —

190

Location of register of debenture holders

Please complete in typescript,
or in bold black capitals.
CHWP000

Company Number

Company Name in full

gives notice that †[a register][registers]†[in duplicate form] of holders of
debentures of the company of the classes mentioned below †[is][are]kept at:

NOTE:
This notice is not
required where the
register is, and has
always been, kept at
the Registered Office

Address

Post town

County / region   Postcode

Brief description of class of debentures

Signed   **Date**

† Please delete as appropriate.

† a director / secretary

You do not have to give any contact
information in the box opposite but
if you do, it will help Companies
House to contact you if there is a
query on the form. The contact
information that you give will be
visible to searchers of the public
record.

Tel

DX number   DX exchange

Companies House receipt date barcode

**This form has been provided free of charge
by Companies House.**

Form revised 10/03

When you have completed and signed the form please send it to the
Registrar of Companies at:
Companies House, Crown Way, Cardiff, CF14 3UZ   DX 33050 Cardiff
for companies registered in England and Wales
or
Companies House, 37 Castle Terrace, Edinburgh, EH1 2EB
for companies registered in Scotland
                                    DX 235 Edinburgh
                                    or LP - 4 Edinburgh 2

Figure A3.7   Notice of a place where a register of holders of debentures or a duplicate is kept or of any change in that place

Companies House
— *for the record* —

325

Location of register of directors' interests in shares etc.

Please complete in typescript,
or in bold black capitals.

CHFP000

Company Number

Company Name in full

The register of directors' interests in shares and/or debentures is kept at:

NOTE:
The register **MUST** be
kept at an address in
the country of
incorporation.

This notice is not
required where the
register is and has
always been kept at the
Registered Office.

Address

Post town

County / Region   **Postcode**

Signed   **Date**

† Please delete as appropriate.

† a director / secretary / administrator / administrative receiver / receiver manager / receiver

Please give the name, address,
telephone number and, if available,
a DX number and Exchange of
the person Companies House should
contact if there is any query.

Tel

DX number   DX exchange

Companies House receipt date barcode

This form has been provided free of charge
by Companies House.

Form revised July 1998

When you have completed and signed the form please send it to the
Registrar of Companies at:
Companies House, Crown Way, Cardiff, CF14 3UZ   DX 33050 Cardiff
for companies registered in England and Wales
or
Companies House, 37 Castle Terrace, Edinburgh, EH1 2EB
for companies registered in Scotland   **DX 235 Edinburgh**

Figure A3.8   Location of register of directors' interests in shares, etc

G

CHFP000

COMPANIES FORM No. 325a

Notice of place for inspection of a register of directors' interests in shares etc. which is kept in a non-legible form, or of any change in that place

325a

Please do not write in this margin

Pursuant to the Companies (Registers and Other Records) Regulations 1985

Note: For use only when the register is kept by computer or in some other non-legible form

Please complete legibly, preferably in black type, or bold block lettering

To the Registrar of Companies
(Address overleaf)

For official use

Company number

Name of company

* insert full name of company

*

gives notice, in accordance with regulation 3(1) of the Companies (Registers and Other Records)

Regulations 1985, that the place for inspection of the register of directors' interests in shares and/or

† delete as appropriate

debentures which the company keeps in a non-legible form is [now] †:

Postcode

† delete as appropriat

Signed

[Director][Secretary]† Date

Presenter's name address and reference (if any) :

For official Use (02/06)
General Section

Post room

Figure A3.9 Notice of a place for inspection of a register of directors' interests in shares, etc, which is kept in a non-legible form, or of any change in that place

Notes

The address for companies registered in England and Wales or Wales is :-

The Registrar of Companies
Companies House
Crown Way
Cardiff
CF14 3UZ

or, for companies registered in Scotland :-

The Registrar of Companies
Companies House
37 Castle Terrace
Edinburgh
EH1 2EB

Figure A3.9 *continued*

G

CHWP000

COMPANIES FORM No. 353a

Notice of place for inspection of a register of members which is kept in a non-legible form, or of any change in that place

353a

Please do not write in this margin

Pursuant to the Companies (Registers and Other Records) Regulations 1985

Note: For use only when the register is kept by computer or in some other non-legible form

Please complete legibly, preferably in black type, or bold block lettering

To the Registrar of Companies
(Address overleaf)

For official use

Company number

Name of company

* insert full name of company

*

gives notice, in accordance with regulation 3(1) of the Companies (Registers and Other Records)

Regulations 1985, that the place for inspection of the register of members of the company which the

† delete as appropriate

company keeps in a non-legible form is [now] †:

Postcode

Signed

[Director][Secretary]† Date

Presenter's name address and reference (if any) :

For official Use (02/06)
General Section

Post room

Figure A3.10   Notice of a place for inspection of a register of members which is kept in a non-legible form, or of any change in that place

Notes

The address for companies registered in England and Wales or Wales is :-

The Registrar of Companies
Companies House
Crown Way
Cardiff
CF14 3UZ
DX 33050 Cardiff

or, for companies registered in Scotland :-

The Registrar of Companies
Companies House
37 Castle Terrace
Edinburgh
EH1 2EB

DX 235 Edinburgh
or LP - 4 Edinburgh 2

Figure A3.10 *continued*

COMPANIES FORM No. 397a

M

CHWP000

**Particulars of an issue of
secured debentures in a series**

397a

Please do not
write in
this margin

Pursuant to section 397 of the Companies Act 1985

Please complete
legibly, preferably
in black type, or
bold block lettering

To the Registrar of Companies
(Address overleaf - Note 3)

For official use

Company number

* insert full name
of Company

Name of company

*

Note
Please read notes
overleaf before
completing this form

Date of present issue

Amount of present issue

Particulars as to commission, allowance or discount (note 2)

Signed _____ Date _____

† delete as
appropriate

On behalf of [company][mortgagee / chargee] †

Presenter's name address and
reference (if any) :

For official Use (02/06)
Mortgage Section

Post room

Time critical reference

Figure A3.11   Particulars of an issue of secured debentures in a series

M

CHWP000

COMPANIES FORM No. 398

**Certificate of registration in
Scotland or Northern Ireland
of a charge comprising property
situate there**

Pursuant to section 398(4) of the Companies Act 1985

398

Please do not
write in
this margin

*Please complete
legibly, preferably
in black type, or
bold block lettering*

To the Registrar of Companies
(Address overleaf)

For official use

Company number

Name of company

* insert full name
of company

*

I

of

* give date and
parties to charge

certify that the charge *

of which a true copy is annexed to this form was presented for registration on

† delete as
appropriate

in [Scotland] [Northern Ireland] †

Signed

Date

Presenter's name address and
reference (if any) :

For official Use (02/06)
Mortgage Section

Post room

Figure A3.12 Certificate of registration in Scotland or Northern Ireland of a charge comprising property situated there

M

CHWP000

COMPANIES FORM No. 403a

**Declaration of satisfaction
in full or in part
of mortgage or charge**

403a

Please do not
write in
this margin

Pursuant to section 403(1) of the Companies Act 1985

*Please complete
legibly, preferably
in black type, or
bold block lettering*

To the Registrar of Companies
(Address overleaf)

For official use

Company number

Name of company

* insert full name
of company

*

I, _____

of _____

† delete as
appropriate

[a director][the secretary][the administrator][the administrative receiver]† of the above company, do
solemnly and sincerely declare that the debt for which the charge described below was given has been
paid or satisfied in **[full][part]**†

insert a description
of the instrument(s)
creating or
evidencing the
charge, eg
'Mortgage',
'Charge',
'Debenture' etc

ø the date of
registration may be
confirmed from the
certificate

Date and description of charge # _____

Date of registration ø _____

Name and address of [chargee][trustee for the debenture holders]† _____

_____

Short particulars of property charged § _____

§ insert brief details
of property

_____

And I make this solemn declaration conscientiously believing the same to be true and by virtue of the
provisions of the Statutory Declarations Act 1835.

Declared at _____

_____

Declarant to sign below

| | Day | Month | Year | |
| on | | | | |

before me _____
A Commissioner for Oaths or Notary Public or Justice of
the Peace or a Solicitor having the powers conferred on a
Commissioner for Oaths.

Presenter's name address and
reference (if any) :

For official Use (02/06)
Mortgage Section

Post room

Figure A3.13 Declaration of satisfaction in full or in part of mortgage
or charge

Notes

The address of the Registrar of Companies is:-

The Registrar of Companies
Companies House
Crown Way
Cardiff
CF14 3UZ

Figure A3.13   *continued*

M

CHWP000

Please do not
write in
this margin

COMPANIES FORM No. 403b

**Declaration that part of the
property or undertaking charged
(a) has been released from the
charge; (b) no longer forms part of
the company's property or undertaking**

403b

Pursuant to section 403(1) (b) of the Companies Act 1985

*Please complete
legibly, preferably
in black type, or
bold block lettering*

To the Registrar of Companies
(Address overleaf)

For official use

Company number

Name of company

* insert full name
of company

*

I, _____

of _____

† delete as
appropriate

[a director][the secretary][the administrator][the administrative receiver]† of the above company, do
solemnly and sincerely declare that with respect to the charge described below the part of the property

insert a description
of the instrument(s)
creating or
evidencing the
charge, eg
"Mortgage",
'Charge',
'Debenture' etc

or undertaking described [has been released from the charge][has ceased to form part of the
company's property or undertaking]†

Date and description of charge # _____

Date of registration ø _____

ø the date of
registration may be
confirmed from the
certificate

Name and address of [chargee][trustee for the debenture holders]† _____

_____

§ insert brief details
of property or
undertaking no
longer subject to
the charge

Short particulars of property or undertaking released or no longer part of the company's property or

undertaking § _____

_____

And I make this solemn declaration conscientiously believing the same to be true and by virtue of the
provisions of the Statutory Declarations Act 1835.

Declared at _____

_____

Declarant to sign below

| | Day | Month | Year | |
on

before me _____
A Commissioner for Oaths or Notary Public or Justice of
the Peace or a Solicitor having the powers conferred on a
Commissioner for Oaths.

Presentor's name address and reference (if any) :	For official Use (02/00) Mortgage Section	Post room

Figure A3.14 Declaration that part of the property or undertaking charged (a) has been released from the charge; (b) no longer forms part of the company's property or undertaking

M

CHWP000

COMPANIES FORM No. 466(Scot)

**Particulars of an instrument of
alteration to a floating charge created
by a company registered in Scotland**

466

A fee of £13 is payable to Companies House in respect of
each register entry for a mortgage or charge.

*Please do not
write in
this margin*

Pursuant to section 410 and 466 of the Companies Act 1985

*Please complete
legibly, preferably
in black type, or
bold block lettering*

To the Registrar of Companies
(Address overleaf - Note 6)

For official use

Company number

Name of company

** insert full name
of company*

*

Date of creation of the charge (note 1)

Description of the instrument creating or evidencing the charge or of any ancillary document which has
been altered (note 1)

Names of the persons entitled to the charge

Short particulars of all the property charged

Presenter's name address and
reference (if any):

For official use (02/06)

Charges Section

Post room

Page 1

Figure A3.15 Particulars of an instrument of alteration to a floating
charge created by a company registered in Scotland

Names, and addresses of the persons who have executed the instrument of alteration (note 2)

Date(s) of execution of the instrument of alteration

A statement of the provisions, if any, imposed by the instrument of alteration prohibiting or restricting the creation by the company of any fixed security or any other floating charge having, priority over, or ranking pari passu with the floating charge

Short particulars of any property released from the floating charge

The amount, if any, by which the amount secured by the floating charge has been increased

Page 2

Figure A3.15   *continued*

A statement of the provisions, if any, imposed by the instrument of alteration varying or otherwise regulating the order of the ranking of the floating charge in relation to fixed securities or to other floating charges

Figure A3.15 *continued*

Continuation of the statement of the provisions, if any, imposed by the instrument of alteration varying or otherwise regulating the order of the ranking of the floating charge in relation to fixed securities or to other floating charges

Please do not write in this margin

Please complete legibly, preferably in black type, or bold block lettering

A fee is payable to Companies House in respect of each register entry for a mortgage or charge.
(See Note 5)

Signed _____ Date _____

On behalf of [company] [chargee]†

Notes

1. A description of the instrument e.g. "Instrument of Charge" "Debenture" etc as the case may be, should be given. For the date of creation of a charge see section 410(5) of the Companies Act.

2. In accordance with section 466(1) the instrument of alteration should be executed by the company, the holder of the charge and the holder of any other charge (including a fixed security) which would be adversely affected by the alteration.

3. A certified copy of the instrument of alteration, together with this form with the prescribed particulars correctly completed must be delivered to the Registrar of Companies within 21 days after the date of execution of that instrument.

4. A certified copy must be signed by or on behalf of the person giving the certification and where this is a body corporate it must be signed by an officer of that body.

5. A fee of £13 is payable to Companies House in respect of each register entry for a mortgage or charge. Cheques and Postal Orders are to be made payable to **Companies House.**

6. The address of the Registrar of Companies is: Companies Registration Office, 37 Castle Terrace, Edinburgh EH1 2EB DX 235 Edinburgh   or   LP - 4 Edinburgh 2

† delete as appropriate

Page 4

Figure A3.15 *continued*

M

CHWP000

COMPANIES FORM No. 419a(Scot)

Application for registration of a memorandum of satisfaction in full or in part of a registered charge

419a

Please do not write in this margin

Pursuant to section 419(1) (a) of the Companies Act 1985

Please complete legibly, preferably in black type, or bold block lettering

To the Registrar of Companies **(Address overleaf)**

Name of company

For official use

Company number

* insert full name of company

*

I, _____

of _____

[a director] [the secretary] [the liquidator] [the receiver] [the administrator]† of the company,

do solemnly and sincerely declare that the debt for which the charge described overleaf was given has been paid or satisfied in **[full] [part]**†

† delete as appropriate

And I make this solemn declaration conscientiously believing the same to be true and by virtue of the provisions of the Statutory Declarations Act 1835.

Declared at _____

_____

_____

Declarant sign below

Day   Month   Year

on

before me _____

A Commissioner for Oaths or Notary Public or Justice of the Peace or Solicitor having the powers conferred on a Commissioner for Oaths

Presenter's name address and reference (if any):

For official use (02/06)

Charges Section

Post room

Page 1

Figure A3.16 Application for registration of a memorandum of satisfaction in full or in part of a registered charge

Particulars of the charge to which the application overleaf refers

Date of creation of the charge

Description of the instrument (if any) creating or evidencing the charge #

Date of Registration *

Short particulars of property charged

Where a FLOATING CHARGE is being satisfied, the following Certificate MUST be completed:

CERTIFICATE

I

of

being [the creditor] [a person authorised to act on behalf of the creditor]† entitled to the benefits of the
floating charge specified above certify that the particulars above relating to the charge and its satisfaction are correct.

Signature _____ Date _____

Note

The address of the Registrar of Companies is:-

Companies House
37 Castle Terrace
Edinburgh
EH1 2EB

DX 235 Edinburgh
or LP - 4 Edinburgh 2

Page 2

Figure A3.16 *continued*

M

CHWP000

Please do not write in this margin

COMPANIES FORM No. 419b(Scot)

Application for registration of a memorandum of fact that part of the property charged (a) has been released from the charge; (b) no longer forms part of the company's property

419b

Pursuant to section 419(1) (b) of the Companies Act 1985

Please complete legibly, preferably in black type, or bold block lettering

To the Registrar of Companies
(Address overleaf)

For official use   Company number

Name of company

* insert full name of company

*

I, _____

of _____

[a director] [the secretary] [the liquidator] [the receiver] [the administrator]† of the company, do solemnly and sincerely declare that the particulars overleaf relating to the charge and the fact that part of the property or undertaking charged [ceased to form part of the company's property or undertaking] [was released from the charge]† on _____ are true to the best of my knowledge and belief.

† delete as appropriate

And I make this solemn declaration conscientiously believing the same to be true and by virtue of the provisions of the Statutory Declarations Act 1835.

Declared at _____   Declarant sign below

_____

on   Day   Month   Year

before me _____

A Commissioner for Oaths or Notary Public or Justice of the Peace or Solicitor having the powers conferred on a Commissioner for Oaths

Presenter's name address and reference (if any):

For official use (02/06)
Charges Section   Post room

Page 1

Figure A3.17 Application for registration of a memorandum of fact that part of the property charged (a) has been released from the charge; (b) no longer forms part of the company's property

Particulars of the charge to which the application overleaf refers

Date of creation of the charge

Description of the instrument (if any) creating or evidencing the charge #

Date of Registration *

Short particulars of property charged

Where a FLOATING CHARGE is being satisfied, the following Certificate MUST be completed:

CERTIFICATE

I _____

of _____

being [the creditor] [a person authorised to act on behalf of the creditor]† entitled to the benefits of the
floating charge specified above certify that the particulars above relating to the charge and the release of part of the
property charged are correct.

Signature _____ Date _____

Note

The address of the Registrar of Companies is:-

Companies House
37 Castle Terrace
Edinburgh
EH1 2EB

DX 235 Edinburgh
or LP - 4 Edinburgh 2

Page 2

Figure A3.17 *continued*

Appendix 4

BOOKS, REGISTERS AND DOCUMENTS WHICH MUST BE AVAILABLE FOR INSPECTION AND OF WHICH COPIES OR EXTRACTS CAN BE REQUISITIONED

Book etc	Who can inspect	Fee	Who can requisition	Time limit for sending	Penalty
Memorandum and Articles	–	–	Any member	Not specified	£400 (company and each officer in default)
Annual Accounts, ie auditors' report, on directors' report, balance sheet and profit and loss account	Copy to all members, debenture holders	None	Members and debenture holders	10 months or within 22 months of incorporation if period covered more than 12 months	Unlimited fine on conviction indictment, £2,000 + £200 daily on summary conviction or £400 +

Book etc	Who can inspect	Fee	Who can requisition	Time limit for sending	Penalty
					£40 daily (company and each officer in default)
*Accounting records	Officers at all times	None	–	–	On indictment 2 years' prison and/or fine; summary conviction 6 months' prison and/or £2,000 fine + £200 daily
Book, vouchers accounts	Auditors at all times	None	–	–	–
	Liquidator	–	–	–	On indictment 7 years' prison and/or fine; summary conviction 6 months' prison and/or £2,000 fine + £200 daily

*To be kept at the registered office or at such other place as the directors designate.
**To be kept at the registered office.

**Charge requiring registration, copy of instrument	Members and creditors	None	–	–	£400 + £40 daily
Directors' service contracts, copies, or notes of their contents	Members	None	–	–	ditto
**Minute book general meeting	Members	None	Members	–	7 days £400 court can make order
**Register of charges	Members, creditors, Anyone else	None / Not exceeding 5p	–	–	£400 + fine £40 daily; court can make order
*Register of debenture holders	Members, debenture holders Anyone else	None / Not exceeding 5p	Anyone	–	ditto
*Register of directors and secretaries	Members Anyone else	None / Not exceeding 5p	–	–	£2,000 fine + £200 daily
**Register of directors' interests	Members Anyone else	None / Not exceeding 5p	Anyone	10 days	£400 + £40 daily
**Register of members and index	Members Anyone else	None / Not exceeding 5p	Members anyone else	Within 10 days of day after receipt of request	£400; court can make order
Special resolution	–	–	Members	Not specified	£400

Book etc	Who can inspect	Fee	Who can requisition	Time limit for sending	Penalty
Extraordinary resolution	–	–	ditto	ditto	ditto
Members' resolution	–	–	ditto	ditto	ditto
Resolution for winding up	–	–	Members	ditto	ditto
Trust deed securing debenture	–	–	Debenture holders	ditto	£400 + £40 daily

Notes:
1. Penalties: Both the company and its officers can be liable for fines.
2. Memorandum: If the Memorandum is altered, the company and officers in default are liable to a fine of £200 in respect of each copy subsequently issued without the amendment.
3. Accounting records: Officers in default have a defence if they acted honestly and the default was excusable in the circumstances, but the records must be retained for at least three years.
4. Books, vouchers and accounts: If records are inadequate or access is denied, this must be stated in the auditors' report.
5. Charges requiring registration: The instrument must be available for inspection during business hours, subject to reasonable restrictions imposed by the company in general meeting, but it must be accessible for at least two hours daily.
6. Directors' service contracts etc, the Minute book, the Register of charges, Register of debenture holders and the Register of directors and secretaries: These must be available on the same basis and the Register of directors' interests must in addition be produced at the Annual General Meeting and remain open and accessible throughout. The Register of members can, however, be closed for not more than 30 days a year, provided notice of closure is advertised in a newspaper local to the registered office.
7. Special resolution and a Resolution for winding up: If the Articles are not registered, a printed copy of the resolution must be filed. If they are registered, the resolution must be annexed to or incorporated in every copy of the Articles issued.

Appendix 5

USEFUL NOTICES AND NOTES

XYZ Limited

Notice is hereby given that the First **Annual General Meeting** of the Company will be held on____day the____day of___20__ at__o'clock in the fore/after noon to transact the following business:

To receive and adopt the Accounts of the Company for the year ended____ together with the Reports of the Directors and the Auditors.

To declare a dividend.

To re-appoint/appoint_____as Auditors of the Company.

To fix the remuneration of the Auditors and to transact any other business which may lawfully be transacted at an Annual General Meeting.

A member entitled to attend and vote at the above meeting may appoint a proxy to attend and vote in his stead. A proxy need not be a member of the company.

By order of the Board

Signed_____

Secretary

Figure A5.1   Notice of Annual General Meeting

XYZ Limited

Notice is hereby given that an **Extraordinary General Meeting** of the above named Company will be held at_____ on ____day the _____day of _____20___ at ____o'clock in the fore/after noon for the purpose of considering and if thought fit passing the Resolution set out   below   which   will   be   proposed   as   an Ordinary/Special/Extraordinary Resolution.

A member entitled to attend and vote at the above meeting may appoint a proxy to attend and on a poll* vote in his stead. A proxy need not be a member of the company.

By order of the Board

Signed _____
Secretary

Resolution

*If the Articles permit a proxy to vote on a show of hands, delete the words 'on a poll'.

Figure A5.2   Notice of meeting

Company number _____

Company name _____

At an **Extraordinary General*/Annual General*/General* Meeting** of the members of the above named Company duly convened and held at:

_____

_____

on the_____day of _____ 20___

the following **Special Resolution** was duly passed:

That the name of the Company be changed to:

(new name) _____

Signature: _____ Chairman, Director, Secretary or Officer of the Company

NB. A copy of the Resolution must be filed with the Registrar within 15 days after the passing of the Resolution.

*Delete as appropriate

Figure A5.3 Special resolution on change of name

Company number _____

Company name _____

We, the undersigned, being all the members of the above Company for the time being entitled to receive notice of, attend and vote at General Meetings, hereby unanimously pass the following resolution and agree that the said resolution shall pass for all purposes be as valid and effective as if the same had been passed at a General Meeting of the Company duly convened and held at:

It is resolved that:

Dated this_____day of _____ 20___

Signed: _____

_____

_____

_____

Figure A5.4 Written resolution

AGREEMENT of MEMBERS to SHORT NOTICE of a GENERAL MEETING and/or of a SPECIAL RESOLUTION

(1) 'I' or 'WE'.
(2) 'Annual' or 'Extraordinary' as the case may be.

(1) _____ the undersigned, being member of the above-named Company and entitled to attend and vote (2) _____ General Meeting of the said Company convened by a Notice of Meeting dated the _____ day of _____ 20 _____ and to be held on the _____ day of _____ 20 _____ , hereby agree that:

1.* The said meeting shall be deemed to have been duly called, notwithstanding that shorter notice than that specified in section 369 of the Companies Act 1985, or in the Company's Articles of Association, has been given therefor.

2.* The copies of the documents referred to in sections 239 and 240 of the Companies Act 1985, which were attached to or enclosed with the said Notice of Meeting, shall be deemed to have been duly sent, notwithstanding that such copies were sent less than twenty-one days before the date of the meeting.

3. The Special Resolution set out in the said Notice of Meeting may be proposed and passed as Special Resolution notwithstanding that such less than twenty-one days' notice of such meeting has been given.

NAME (in block capitals)	ADDRESS	SIGNATURE†

NOTES

• Delete this paragraph if not required.

† The documents referred to are the company's profit and loss account and balance sheet, the directors' report, the auditors' report and, where the Company has subsidiaries and section 229 applies, the Company's group accounts.

‡(a) In the case where agreement is required only to the holding of an Extraordinary General Meeting, and/or to the passing of Special Resolutions at an Extraordinary General Meeting, on short notice, agreement must be given by a majority in number of the members having a right to attend and vote at the meeting, being a majority together holding not less than 95 per cent in nominal value of the shares giving a right to attend and vote at the meeting, or, in the case of a company not having a share capital, together representing not less than 95 per cent of the total voting rights at the meeting of all the members.

(b) In any other case, agreement must be given by all the members entitled to attend and vote at the meeting.

(c) One form may be signed by all the members concerned, or several similar forms may be signed by one or more of them.

Figure A5.5 Agreements of members to short notice of a general meeting and/or of a special resolution

Section 369 (3) and *(4)* of the Companies Act 1985 provide as follows:

(3) Notwithstanding that a meeting is called by shorter notice than that specified in subsection (2) or in the company's articles (as the case may be), it is deemed to have been duly called if it is so agreed:

  (a) in the case of a meeting called as the annual general meeting, by all the members entitled to attend and vote at it; and

  (b) otherwise, by the requisite majority.

(4) The requisite majority for this purpose is a majority in number of the members having a right to attend and vote at the meeting, being a majority:

  (a) together holding not less than 95 per cent in nominal value of the shares giving a right to attend and vote at the meeting; or

  (b) in the case of a company not having a share capital, together representing not less than 95 per cent of the total voting rights at that meeting of all the members.

Section 378 (2) and *(3)* of the Companies Act 1985 provide as follows:

(2) A resolution is a special resolution when it has been passed by such a majority as is required for the passing of an extraordinary resolution and at a general meeting of which not less than 21 days' notice, specifying the intention to propose the resolution as a special resolution, has been duly given.

(3) If it is so agreed by a majority in number of the members having the right to attend and vote at such a meeting, being a majority:

  (a) together holding not less than 95 per cent in nominal value of the shares giving that right; or

  (b) in the case of a company not having a share capital, together representing not less than 95 per cent of the total voting rights at that meeting of all the members,

  a resolution may be proposed and passed as a special resolution at a meeting of which less than 21 days' notice has been given.

Section 239 of the Companies Act 1985 provides as follows:

For the purposes of this Part, a company's accounts for a financial year are to be taken as comprising the following documents:

  (a) the company's profit and loss account and balance sheet,

  (b) the directors' report,

  (c) the auditors' report, and

  (d) where the company has subsidiaries and section 229 applies, the company's group accounts.

Section 240 of the Companies Act 1985 provides as follows:

(1) In the case of every company, a copy of the company's accounts for the financial year shall, not less than 21 days before the date of the meeting at which they are to be laid in accordance with the next section, be sent to each of the following persons:

    (a) every member of the company (whether or not entitled to receive notice of general meetings),

    (b) every holder of the company's debenture (whether or not so entitled), and

    (c) all persons other than members and debenture holders, being persons so entitled.

(2) In the case of a company not having a share capital, subsection (1) does not require a copy of the accounts to be sent to a member of the company who is not entitled to receive notices of general meetings of the company, or to a holder of the company's debentures who is not so entitled.

(3) Subsection (1) does not require copies of the accounts to be sent:

    (a) to a member of the company or a debenture holder, being in either case a person who is not entitled to receive notices of general meetings, and of whose address the company is unaware, or

    (b) to more than one of the joint holders of any shares or debentures none of whom are entitled to receive such notices, or

    (c) in the case of joint holders of shares or debentures some of whom are, and some not, entitled to receive such notices, to those who are not so entitled.

(4) If copies of the accounts are sent less than 21 days before the date of the meeting, they are, notwithstanding that fact, deemed to have been duly sent if it is so agreed by all the members entitled to attend and vote at the meeting.

Obligation to print certain documents

The Companies Act 1985

The European Communities Act 1972

1. The following documents are required to be printed:

    (a) Articles of Association

    (b) Altered Memorandums of Association

    (c) Altered Articles of Association

2. The Registrar of Companies is prepared to regard the printing stipulation as satisfied by the following processes:
Letterpress, Gravure, Lithography.
Stencil duplicating, Offset lithography, 'Office' typeset.
Electrostatic photocopying.
'Photostat' or similar processes properly processed and washed.
Stencil duplicating, using wax stencils and black ink.

3. The following documents when submitted for registration must be either printed or in a form approved by the Registrar:
   (a) Ordinary Resolutions increasing the capital of any company.
   (b) Special and Extraordinary Resolutions and Agreements as specified in section 380 of the Companies Act 1985.
   The Registrar is prepared to accept for registration such copy Resolutions and Agreements if produced by a process named in paragraph 2 above or by spirit duplicator, of if typed.

4. No document will be accepted if it is illegible. Where it is considered that a document, though legible, cannot be reproduced to an adequate standard for presentation to the public in microfiche or photocopy form, the Registrar's practice is to seek the cooperation of the presentor in providing a clearer copy.

5. The Registrar's present practice is to accept copies of the Memorandum and Articles amended in accordance with the following rules:
   Where the amendment is small in extent, eg a change of name or a change in the nominal capital, a copy of the original document may be amended by rubber stamp, 'top copy' typing or in some other permanent manner (but not a manuscript amendment).
   An alteration of a few lines or a complete short paragraph may be similarly dealt with if the new version is satisfactorily permanently affixed to a copy of the original in such a way as to obscure the amended words.
   Where more substantial amendments are involved, the pages amended may be removed from a copy of the original, the amended text inserted and the pages securely collated. The inserted material must be 'printed' as defined above but need not be produced by the same process as the original.
   In all cases the alterations must be validated by the seal or an official stamp of the company.

6. Where the document is produced other than by letterpress, a certificate by the printer stating the process used must be endorsed on or accompany the document.

7. It has been found the experience that documents produced by semi-dry developed dye line (diazo) copies produced by spirit duplicating or thermo-copying do not satisfy the general conditions.

COMPANIES ACTS

Elective Resolution
(Pursuant to section 379A of the Companies Act 1985)

Company number _____

Company name _____

At an Extraordinary General Meeting of the above-named company duly convened and held at:

_____

_____

on the_____day of _____ 20___

the following Elective Resolution was duly passed:

It is resolved that:

Signed: _____

NOTE: to be filed within 15 days of passing the Resolution.

Figure A5.6 Elective resolution

Section 379A of the Companies Act 1985 provides as follows:

(1) An election by a private company for the purposes of:
  (a) section 80A (election as to duration of authority to allot shares);
  (b) section 252 (election to dispense with laying of accounts and reports before general meeting);
  (c) section 366A (election to dispense with holding of annual general meeting);
  (d) section 369 (4) or 378 (3) (election as to majority required to authorise short notice of meeting);

or

  (e) section 386 (election to dispense with appointment of auditors annually), shall be made by resolution of the company in general meeting in accordance with this section. Such a resolution is referred to in this Act as an 'elective resolution'.

(2) An elective resolution is not effective unless:
  (a) at least 21 days' notice in writing is given of the meeting, stating that an elective resolution is to be proposed and stating the terms of the resolution; and
  (b) the resolution is agreed to at the meeting, in person or by proxy, by all the members entitled to attend and vote at the meeting.

(3) The company may revoke an elective resolution by passing an ordinary resolution to that effect.

(4) An elective resolution shall cease to have effect if the company is re-registered as a public company.

(5) An elective resolution may be passed or revoked in accordance with this section and the provisions referred to in subsection (1) have effect notwithstanding any contrary provision in the company's Articles of Association.

NOTE: The Registrar of Companies is prepared to accept copy resolutions or agreements if produced to a standard which is legible and can be reproduced to an adequate standard for presentation to the public in microfiche or photocopied format. Signatures must, however, be original and not photocopied.

Widgets Limited

I, _____ of _____

being a member of the above named Company and entitled to vote

hereby appoint _____ of _____

or him failing _____ of _____

as my proxy to attend and vote for me and on my behalf at the Annual/Extraordinary General Meeting of the Company to be held

on _____ day the _____ day of _____ Two thousand

and _____, and at any adjournment thereof

As witness My hand this _____ day of _____ 20___

Signed _____

in the presence of _____ *

This proxy must be deposited at the Registered Office of the Company not less than _____ hours before the time fixed for holding the above mentioned meeting

NB. Any alterations made to the form must be initialled by the signatory and the witness

*If the Company's Articles require the signature to be witnessed, the witness should write in his name, address and occupation.

Figure A5.7 Form of proxy

Appendix 6

USEFUL ADDRESSES

British Business Angels Association
5th Floor, 52–54 Southwark Street
London SE1 1UN
Tel: 020 7089 2305
Website: www.bbaa.org.uk

British Chambers of Commerce
Manning House
22 Carlisle Place
London SW1P 1JA
Tel: 020 7565 2000
Website: www.britishchambers.org.uk

British Insurance Brokers Association
BIBA House
14 Bevis Marks
London EC3A 7NT
Tel: 020 7623 9043
Website: www.biba.org.uk

British Venture Capital Association
3 Clements Inn
London WC2A 2AZ
Tel: 020 7025 2950
Website: www.bvcc.co.uk

Business Link
National Contact Centre: 0845 600 9006
Website: www.businesslink.org
(There are also numerous local Business Links)

Capital Taxes Office England and Wales
Ferrers House
PO Box 38
Castle Meadow Road
Nottingham NG2 1BB
Tel: 0115 974 2400
Website: www.inlandrevenue.gov.uk.cto

Northern Ireland
Level 3, Dorchester House
52–58 Great Victoria Street
Belfast BT2 7QL
Tel: 028 9050 5353

Scotland
Meldrum House
15 Drumshengh Gardens
Edinburgh EH3 7UG
Tel: 0131 777 4050

Central Office of Information
Hercules House
Hercules Road
London SE1 7DU
Tel: 020 7928 2345
Website: coi.gov.uk

Chartered Association of Certified Accountants
29 Lincoln's Inn Fields
London WC2A 3EE
Tel: 020 7396 5800
Website: www.accaglobal.com

Chartered Institute of Arbitrators
12 Bloomsbury Square
London WC1A 2LP
Tel: 020 7421 7444
Website: www.arbritrators.org

Chartered Institute of Management Accountants
63 Portland Place
London W1N 4AB
Tel: 020 7917 9277
Website: www.cimaglobal.com

Companies House

The telephone number for all branches is 0870 33 33 363, and the website is
www.companieshouse.gov.uk

Cardiff:
Crown Way
Maindy Cardiff CF14 3UZ

London:
21 Bloomsbury Street
London WC1B 32XD

Birmingham:
Central Library
Chamberlain Square
Birmingham B3 3HQ

Leeds:
25 Queen Street
Leeds LS1 2TW

Manchester:
75 Mosley Street
Manchester M2 3HR

Edinburgh:
37 Castle Terrace
Edinburgh EH1 2EB

Competition Commission, The
New Court
48 Carey Street
London WC2A 2JT
Tel: 020 7271 0100
Website: www.competition-commission.gov.uk

Confederation of British Industry (CBI)
Centre Point
New Oxford Street
London WC1A 1DU
Tel: 020 7379 7400
Website: www.cbl.org.uk

Consumer Credit Trade Association
Suite 8
The Wool Exchange
10 Hustlergate
Bradford BD1 1RE
Tel: 01274 390380

Department for Education and Skills
The Sanctuary Buildings
Great Smith Street
London SW1P 3BT
Tel: 0870 000 2288
E-mail: info@dfes.gsi.gov.uk
Website: www.dfes.gov.uk

Department of Trade and Industry
1 Victoria Street
London SW1H 0ET
Tel: 020 7215 5000
Website: www.dti.gov.uk

European Patent Office
Erhardtstrasse 27 8033
Munich
Germany
Tel: 4989 23990
Website: www.european-patent-office.org

Export Credits Guarantee Department
2 Exchange Tower
PO Box 2200
Harbour Exchange Square
London E14 9GS
Tel: 020 7512 7000
Website: www.ecgd.gov.uk

Finance and Leasing Association
15–19 Kingsway
London WC2B 6UN
Tel: 020 7836 6511
Website: www.fla.org.uk

H M Revenue and Customs
Tax and VAT information and services online at www.hmrc.gov.uk,
including addresses and telephone numbers of local offices.

Information Commissioner's Office
Head Office
Wycliffe House
Water Lane
Wilmslow
Cheshire SK9 5 AF
Tel: 01625 545 745
Website: www.ico.gov.uk

Regional offices
Information Commissioner's Office – Scotland
28 Thistle Street
Edinburgh EH2 1EN
Tel: 0131 225 6341

Information Commissioner's Office – Wales
1 Alexandra Gate
Ffordd Pengam
Cardiff CF24 2SA
Tel: 02920 894 929

Information Commissioner's Office – Northern Ireland
Room 101, Regus House
33 Clarendon Dock
Laganside
Belfast BT1 3BG
Tel: 028 9051 1270

Institute of Chartered Accountants in England and Wales
PO Box 433
Moorgate Place
London EC2P 2BJ
Tel: 020 7920 8100
Website: www.icaew.co.uk

Institute of Chartered Accountants in Ireland
87–89 Pembroke Road
Dublin 4
Republic of Ireland
Tel: 00 3531 637 7200
Website: www.iacai.ie

Institute of Chartered Accountants of Scotland
CA House
21 Haymarket Yards
Edinburgh EH12 5BH
Tel: 0131 347 0100
Website: www.icas.org.uk

Institute of Chartered Secretaries and Administrators
16 Park Crescent
London W1N 4AH
Tel: 020 7580 4741
Website: www.icsa.org.uk

Institute of Directors
116 Pall Mall
London SW1Y 5ED
Tel: 020 7839 1233
Website: www.iod.com

Institute of Management
Management House
Cottingham Road
Corby
Northamptonshire NN17 1TT
Tel: 01536 204222
Website: www.inst.mgt.org.uk

Insurance Ombudsman Bureau
The Financial Ombudsman Service
South Quay Plaza
183 Marsh Wall
London E14 9SR
Tel: 0845 080 1800
Website: www.theiob.org.uk

International Chamber of Commerce
14–15 Belgrave Square
London SW1X 8PS
Tel: 020 7823 2811
Website: iccuk.net

Land Charges Registry
The Superintendent Land Charges Department
DX 8249
Plumer House
Tailyour Road
Crownhill
Plymouth PL6 5HY
Tel: 01752 635600
Website: landreg.gov.uk
(There are 24 Land Registries in England and Wales)

Law Society, The
113 Chancery Lane
London WC2A 1PL
Tel: 020 7242 1222
Website: www.lawsociety.org.uk

Learning and Skills Council
Cheylesmore House
Quinton Road
Coventry CV1 2WT
Tel: 0845 019 4170
Website: www.lsc.gov.uk

London Chamber of Commerce
33 Queen Street
London EC4R 1AD
Tel: 020 7248 4444
Website: www.londonchamber.co.uk
(Business Registry offers free advice and search facilities to members)

London Gazette
PO Box 7923
London SE1 5ZH
Tel: 020 7394 4580
Website: www.london-gazette.co.uk

Office of Fair Trading
Fleetbank House
2-6 Salisbury Square
London EC4Y 8JX
Tel: 020 7211 8000
Website: www.oft.gov.uk

The Patent Office
Concept House
Cardiff Road
Newport
South Wales NP10 8QQ
Tel: 08459 500 505
Website: www.patent.gov.uk

Register of Judgments, Orders and Fines
171–173 Cleveland Street
London W1P 5PE
Tel: 020 7380 0133
Website: www.registry-trust.org.uk

The Office of Public Sector Information/Her Majesty's Stationery Office (HMSO)
St Crispins
Duke Street
Norwich NR3 1PD
Tel: 0870 600 5522
Website: www.opsi.gov.uk

Trade Marks Registry
The Patent Office
Cardiff Road
Newport
Gwent NP9 1RH
Tel: 01633 814000

CONTACT INFORMATION FOR ADVERTISERS

1st Contact
Castlewood House
77–91 New Oxford Street
London WC1A 1DJ
Tel: 0800 082 0659
E-mail: assistance@1stcontact.co.uk
Website: www.1stcontact.co.uk

24 Hour Business
441 Gateford Road
Worksop
Nottinghamshire SB1 7BN
Tel: 08000 470 270
Websites: www.24hrbusiness.co.uk
www.clickpayroll.co.uk

AA Thornton & Co
29 St Katherines Street
Northampton NN1 2QZ
Tel: 01604 638 242
E-mail: aat@aathornton.com
Website: www.aathornton.com

Angel Finance & Property Services
F32 Waterfront Studios
Royal Victoria Docks
1 Dock Road
London E16 1AG
Tel: 020 7474 4242

Beck Greener
Fulwood House
12 Fulwood Place
London WC1V 6HR
Contact: Jonathan Silverman
Tel: 020 7693 5600
E-mail: mail@beckgreener.com
Website: www.beckgreener.com

Business Gateways Ltd
7 Troymede
Balcombe
West Sussex RH17 6LU
Tel: 0800 328 9784
E-mail: advice@getfactoring.com
Website: www.getfactoring.com

**Charterhouse Commercial
   Finance plc**
Bourne Concourse
Peel Street
Ramsey
Isle of Man IMB 1JJ
and
Oakfield House
35 Perrymount Rd
Haywards Heath
West Sussex RH16 3BW
Tel: 0870 243 1836
E-mail:
sales@charterhousefactoring.com
Website:
www.charterhousefactoring.com

Coddan CPM Ltd
5 Percy Street
London W1T 1DG
Tel: 020 7748 3039 / 0800 081 1510
E-mail: info@ukincorp.co.uk
Website: www.ukincorp.co.uk

The Company Wizard
Orchard Business Centre
Orchard Street
Swansea SA1 5AS
Tel: 0870 766 8301
Website:
www.CompanyWizard.co.uk

**Cranleys Chartered
  Accountants**
Advice Centre
24 Finns Business Park
Mill Lane
Crondall
Farnham
Surrey GU10 5RX
Contact: Colin Davidson
Tel: 01252 852 220
Website: www.cranleys.co.uk

DFK UK
Russell Square House
10–12 Russell Square
London WC1B 5LF

Scotland:
Sandy Mowat
Tel: 0141 354 0354
E-mail: smowat@dfkuk.com

North England:
John Richards
Tel: 0191 256 9500
E-mail: jrichards@dfkuk.com

North West and East:
James White
Tel: 0113 246 1234
E-mail: jwhite@dfkuk.com

Midlands:
Steven Heathcote
Tel: 0121 454 4141
E-mail: sheathcote@dfkuk.com

South West and South Wales:
Steve Fox
Tel: 01225 428 114
E-mail: sfox@dfkuk.com

London and South East:
Mark Lamb
Tel: 0207 509 9000
E-mail: mlamb@dfkuk.com

East Anglia:
Peter Gardiner
Tel: 01206 549 303
E-mail: pgardiner@dfkuk.com

South Coast:
Neil Raynsford
Tel: 023 8061 3000
E-mail: nraynsford@dfkuk.com

Isle of Man:
Gethin Taylor
Tel: 01624 647 171
E-mail: gtaylor@dfkuk.com

Jersey:
Peter Nicolle
Tel: 01534 488 000
E-mail: pnicolle@dfkuk.com

Ireland:
James O'Connor
Tel: +353 (1) 6790 800
E-mail: joconnor@dfkuk.com

Formations Direct
39a Leicester Road
Salford M7 4AS
Tel: 0800 6300 316
Website:
www.formationsdirect.com

Forrester Ketley & Co
North London:
Forrester House
52 Bounds Green Road
London N11 2EY
Tel: 020 8889 6622

Central London:
6th Floor
105 Piccadilly
London W1J 7NJ
Tel: 020 8889 6622

Birmingham:
Chamberlain House
Paradise Place
Birmingham B3 3HP
Tel: 0121 236 0484
E-mail: info@forresters.co.uk
Website: www.forresters.co.uk

Frank B Dehn & Co
St Bride's House
10 Salisbury Square
London EC4Y 8JD
Tel: 020 7632 7200
E-mail: info@frankbdehn.com
Website: www.frankbdehn.com

Hanover Company Services
44 Upper Belgrave Road
Clifton
Bristol BS8 2XN
Tel: 0800 068 5362
Website: www.hanovercs.com

HGF / HGF-Law
Belgrave Hall
Belgrave Street
Leeds LS2 8DD
Contact: Cristina Rivas Graver
Tel: 0113 233 0106
E-mail: crgraver@hgf.com

HSBC Bank plc
Level 31
8 Canada Square
Canary Wharf
London E14 5HQ
Tel: 0800 633 5610
Website:
www.hsbc.com/commercial

ICAEW
(The Institute of Chartered
   Accountants in England & Wales)
Chartered Accountants Hall
PO Box 433
Moorgate Place
London EC2P 2BJ
Website: www.icaew.co.uk/find

Labyrinth Technology
Unit 34
The City Business Centre
Lower Road
London SE16 2XB
Tel: 08707 66 23 27
E-mail: QBH@labyrinthIT.co.uk
Websites:
www.CommsHeaven.com
www.QuickBooksHeaven.com

Lawyers for Your Business
7th Floor, Fox Court
14 Grays Inn Road
London WC1X 8HN
Tel: 080 7405 9075
E-mail: lfyb@lawsociety.org.uk
Website:
www.lfyb.lawsociety.org.uk

**Lubbock Fine Chartered
   Accountants**
Russell Bedford House
City Forum
250 City Road
London EC1V 2QQ
Contact: Mark Turner
Tel: 020 7490 7766
E-mail:
markturner@lubbockfine.co.uk
Website: www.lubbockfine.co.uk

The Patent Office
Room 1L 01
Cardiff Road
Newport
South Wales NP10 8QQ
Tel: 08459 500 505
Website: www.patent.gov.uk

Premierline Direct
Premierline Direct Limited
PO Box 640
Lancaster LA1 3XD
Tel: 0800 058 2226
Website:
www.premierlinedirect.co.uk

Prentice & Matthews
Calvert's Buildings
52B Borough High Street
London SE1 1XN
Tel: 020 7403 8565
E-mail: info@prenmatt.co.uk
Website: www.prenmatt.co.uk

Stonemartin
New Broad Street House
35 New Broad Street
London EC2M 1NH
Contact: Tim Worboys
Tel: 020 7194 7503 / 0845 070 9970
Website: www.stonemartin.com

Index

NB: page numbers in *italic* indicate figures or tables

Index of advertisers